EASTERN PSYCHOLOGY

Buddhism, Hinduism, and Taoism

WILLIAM COMPTON PH.D.

ISBN: 146649462X
ISBN 13: 9781466494626

Library of Congress Control Number: 2011960075
CreateSpace, North Charleston, SC

To Barbara,
a bodhisattva who consents
to share her life with me.

Contents

Preface

Learn from the ancient ones, and
Learn from those of foreign lands.

OLD CHINESE PROVERB[1]

This book will present a brief overview of the psychological theories and practices found in Buddhism, Hinduism, and Taoism. The book is written for both students of psychology and anyone who has an interest in Eastern psychology. I have tried to create a book that is accurate and informative, while keeping it readable and accessible to as many people as possible. I have also included many references to books and articles by Western psychologists who have studied Eastern thought and practiced Eastern disciplines. I hope the focus on these authors will provide more easily accessible information to any reader who wishes to pursue these ideas further.

The book is the result of my 40-year plus fascination with Eastern wisdom and Eastern psychology. It began in 1966 when I was a freshman at the University of Wisconsin at Madison. At the time, I took a course titled "Wisdom Literature" taught by Mr. Willard Johnson, who was then a graduate student in the Far Eastern Studies program at the university (one of his later books can be found in the bibliograph). In that class, I discovered ideas on wisdom and well-being from Buddhism, Hinduism, Taoism, Zen, and other Eastern perspectives. The book "The Way of Zen" by Alan Watts, who for many years was the

---

1   From *Yoga and Psychotherapy: The Evolution of Consciousness* by Swami Rama, Rudolph Ballentine, and Swami Ajaya (1975), Himalayan Institute Press, pg. *xx*.

major interpreter of Eastern wisdom for the general public, especially struck me. The ideas seemed to resonate with me; I knew there was real wisdom in these writings. It was also apparent to me that I could only glimpse the depths of knowledge contained in these texts. I began a brief academic exploration of these topics as a Far Eastern Studies major at the university.

A few years later, however, I found myself searching for a discipline that would acknowledge these ideas and put them into a more practical framework for Western audiences. I believed that Western psychology would provide such a framework. Sadly, I discovered that in the academic world of 1975 most Western psychologists rejected ideas from Eastern psychology. However, as a student I was also lucky enough to find mentors that encouraged my interests. Dr. Thomas B. Roberts at Northern Illinois University and Dr. Gordon Becker at the University of Nebraska at Omaha allowed me to explore both the theoretical and practical explorations of Eastern psychology.

Today the situation in Western psychology is quite different than what I found over 45 years ago. Practical applications such as meditation, yoga, tai chi chuan, and mindfulness are found in many areas of Western psychology, especially in clinical and counseling psychology. Even a few theoretical perspectives from Eastern psychology can be found in studies of cognition, attention, and emotion. Nonetheless, Western psychology still taps into only a few ideas from an Eastern perspective on psychology. In addition, the basic foundations of Eastern psychology are often totally ignored when the practical techniques are adopted in the West. I hope this book will help fill a few of the gaps that still exist between an Eastern and a Western approach to psychology.

The topic of Eastern psychology is an enormous one that I approach with no small amount of fear and trembling. After all, I am a psychologist and not a formally trained scholar of Far East Asian religion and philosophy. Therefore, I have chosen topics that I believe would be interesting to students and professionals in psychology. It should come as no surprise that most of the ideas presented here only scratch the surface and many scholars have spent a lifetime investigating only one of these topics.

The history of Eastern psychology extends back at least 5,000 years and over that time many different interpretations of basic ideas have evolved. Since the amount of information on Buddhism, Hinduism, and Taoism is absolutely enormous, I have also presented a focused journey through these topics. Some type of focus is absolutely necessary in a book such as this one that presents a general survey of numerous traditions. Some choices simply had to be made concerning how to present the ideas. For instance, in Buddhist psychology there is the concept of "the realms of rebirth", which are often depicted in Tibetan mandalas. Some traditions say there are six realms and other traditions combine two of these to create five realms. Out of necessity, I had to choose which to present in the book. When making that choice, as well as others, I tried to guide my selection by looking at presentations that were used more frequently or that might be more familiar to Western readers. In addition, the topics I choose to discuss are those that I believe would be of interest to psychologists, especially those that seem to point out the unique contrasts between Eastern and Western ideas.

I must include a note about the spellings and technical terms in the book. Terms used in Hinduism are almost always written in Sanskrit, which was the language of the Brahmin priests during the Vedic period when major texts of Hinduism were written down. Terms in Sanskrit are *italicized* in the text. Buddhism can also use terms from Sanskrit, but frequently refers to the same concepts using spellings found in Pali. For the first few hundred years after the Buddha's death, his words were passed down through the oral tradition. When they were finally written down the texts that are the most widely known today were those written in Pali. In the book, a "*P*" in parentheses or italics after a word indicates it comes from Pali. Terms used in Tibetan Buddhism can come from Sanskrit, Pali, or Tibetan. In order to avoid too much confusion in the book, Tibetan words will be used infrequently. Words used to describe Taoist concepts are familiar Westernized translations of Chinese terms. Recently, many Chinese have begun to use spellings for Taoist names and concepts that are more consistent with the Chinese language. However, since this book is for Western readers, the older and more familiar spellings were retained.

Many terms in Sanskrit, Pali, Tibetan, and Chinese will contain diacritical marks when written for Western readers. Frequently these marks will change depending on the work in which they appear. Therefore, in order to avoid too much confusion, I have omitted most diacritical marks from the text. While I hope this exclusion facilitates the reading experience, those who explore these ideas further will find diacritical marks are included in some of the sources cited in the bibliography.

I would like to thank a number of people who have helped me with this book. First, my nephew Dave Compton gave editorial help and provided feedback on the content. Second, I am extremely grateful to John Whiteman for working his PhotoShop magic on some of my photographs. Third, a number of people helped with references and other tedious, but necessary, sections of a book: Hester Wei Ralph, Tori Counts, Laura Kloster, Ranger Tillman, and Courtney Allison. Third, I would also like to thank the Committee on Non-Instructional Assignment at Middle Tennessee State University for granting a sabbatical leave so I could begin this book. A big thanks you to the folks at CreateSpace publishing for their help with the preparation of the manuscript.

A big heartfelt "thank you!" goes out to reviewers who gave me very helpful feedback on the initial drafts of the manuscript: Ralph Hood Jr., Ph.D. of the University of Tennessee at Chattanooga, Swami Allan Ajaya, Ph.D., and Susan Schoenbohm, Ph.D. of Vanderbilt University. The book is so much better because of their assistance. I'd also like to thank my meditation teachers: Dainin Katagiri-Roshi, Trudy Goodman, and George Bowman, as well a number of other teachers I have met along the way. Finally, thanks to Rusty Rust for tai chi chuan.

Acknowledgments and Permissions

I would like to thank the following for graciously allowing me to use figures, tables, and photos that appear in the book:

Cover Painting	White Lotus with Cobalt by Lisa Ernst: www.lisaernst.com Used with permission.
Figure 3.1	Illustration on page 67, from the book The Seven Systems of Eastern Philosophy by Pandit Rajmani Tigunait, copyright ©, 1983 by the Himalayan International Institute of Yoga Science and Philosophy of the U.S. A. Reprinted with permission of Himalayan Institute Press, 1-800-822-4547, www.HimalayanInstitute.org.
Figure 3.2	From Alchemy: Science of the Cosmos, Science of the Soul by Titus Burkhardt, copyright © 1997, Fons Vitae Publishing & Distribution, 49 Mockingbird Valley Drive, Louisville, KY, USA, www.fonsvitae.com. Used with permission.
Figure 3.3	The "Wheel of Life" painting is a representation of a wall painting exhibited in the Spiritual Theater of the Wat Suan Mokkh Buddhist monastery in Surat Thani, Thailand. Used with permission.
Figure 3.4	From The Tantric Mysticism of Tibet by John Blofeld, copyright © 1970, George Allen and Unwin Ltd. Used by permission of Dutton, a division of Penguin Group (USA), Inc.
Figure 3.5	From The Essence of Tao by Pamela Ball, copyright © 2004, Arcturus Publications/Eagle editions, London. Used with permission.
Table 4.2	Material adapted from: Daniel Goleman (1975). Primary mental health factors in classical Buddhist psychology. Journal of Transpersonal Psychology, 7(2), pgs. 176–181. Used with permission.

Photo 2.1	Kwan-yin, the bodhisattva of compassion. Property of/photo by the author.
Photo 2.2	Nataraj, the dancing form of Lord Shiva. Photo by Michael Emrick. Property of William Hollings. Used with permission.
Photo 2.3	Manjusri, the bodhisattva of transcendental wisdom. Property of/photo by the author.
Photo 5.1	Gallen Priory Cross representation made by the Wild Goose Studio in Kinsale, Ireland. Property of/photo by the author.

Every effort has been made to trace all copyright holders, but if any have been inadvertently overlooked, the author and publisher will be pleased to make the necessary arrangements at the first opportunity.

CHAPTER 1

Introduction To Eastern Psychology

> I think that the very purpose of life is to seek happiness. That is clear. Whether one believes in religion or not...we are all seeking something better in life. So, I think, the very motion of our life is toward happiness.
>
> HIS HOLINESS THE 14TH DALAI LAMA[1]

L ate in the nineteenth century, Rudyard Kipling wrote, "East is East, and West is West, and never the twain shall meet, till earth and sky stand presently at God's great judgment seat."[2] Kipling was referring to the sense of curiosity, confusion, and often bewilderment that most Westerners of his time felt toward the cultures of the East. If people in Kipling's world had any contact with cultures of the East (such as those of India, China, Tibet, or Japan), then the customs, fashions, art, and philosophies of those places seemed so completely different, so utterly foreign, that finding common ground appeared almost impossible.

Today this situation is quite different in many ways, and yet quite similar as well. Most people in the Western world are familiar with practices from the East, such as yoga, meditation, tai chi chuan, or martial arts. In fact, many people in the West are dedicated practitioners of these disciplines. In this sense, the situation today is different than it was in Kipling's day. On the other hand, many people in the West are still unfamiliar with the psychological and philosophical foundations that have supported these practices for thousands of years. This book is designed to introduce the reader to the basic psychological foundations that inform meditative practices from the East. First, a small clarification is necessary. The term *Eastern psychology* can have a number of meanings. In this book, the term *Eastern psychology* will refer to the psychological systems found within Hinduism, Buddhism, and Taoism (pronounced DOW-*ism*).

Systems of eastern psychology offer some of the oldest perspectives on psychology, because the roots of eastern psychology are deeply embedded in humankind's oldest religious traditions. The origins of yoga in India go back 5,000 years and predate written historical records. The written origins of Taoism in China can be found almost 3,000 years ago, beginning sometime around 700 BCE. Buddhism began with the teachings of the Buddha in approximately 530 BCE.[3] The core elements of the Eastern perspectives on psychology have been remarkably consistent for thousands of years.

Although interest in meditation, yoga, tai chi chuan, acupuncture, and other techniques from the East has grown in the Western world, these techniques have frequently been applied in psychology without actually understanding the cultural assumptions that helped create and sustain these practices in their native cultures. For instance, martial arts have often been taught in the West simply as methods of combat, while the spiritual foundations of the disciplines are not mentioned or taught. Similarly, practices involving sexuality in tantra are frequently taken out the original spiritual context and taught simply as methods to enhance sensual pleasure. Only recently has Western psychology begun to seriously investigate how cultural assumptions about social relationships, the nature of self, and mental health have led to misinterpretation of ideas from different cultures and contributed to creating cultural bias in current psychological theories.[4] For instance, this cultural bias has been seen when Western mental health professionals misinterpreted certain very dramatic experiences during meditation as symptoms of schizophrenia or brief psychosis.

The first section of this chapter will present a few of the major ideas that distinguish the Eastern systems of psychology. Particular attention will be paid to those ideas that may be in contrast to how psychology is viewed in the West.[5] The last section of the chapter will present a very brief historical overview of Hinduism, Buddhism, and Taoism.

FOUNDATIONS OF EASTERN PSYCHOLOGY

PSYCHOLOGY, PHILOSOPHY, AND RELIGION

The first core idea that distinguishes Eastern from Western psychology is that the Eastern perspectives are embedded in the religious traditions of the East. That is, the basic principles of Eastern psychology are found in the core beliefs of Eastern religions, primarily Hinduism, Buddhism, and Taoism. So, while western psychology has struggled to differentiate itself from religion, the Eastern psychologies are inseparable from the Eastern religions. This is in part because Eastern thinkers never deemed it necessary to divide the human psyche into separate disciplines for religion, psychology, and philosophy. For instance, the fact that Buddhism is simultaneously a religion, a philosophical system, and a system of personality transformation challenges the usual categories used to separate these areas of knowledge in the West. ★

The primary reason that the psychological, philosophical, and religious systems of the East are so intertwined is because they all share the same goal. All attempt to help people lead lives that are happy, fulfilling, and provide the deepest possible sense of well-being and inner peace. From the perspective of Eastern psychology, the only way to achieve an ultimate sense of peace or psychological well-being is to gain insight into a deeper spiritual reality. The pursuit of lasting happiness and psychological liberation from suffering is intimately tied to a spiritual quest. Further, in the East, all of the avenues of inquiry are grounded in personal spiritual experiences. Therefore, when the Hindu yogi says that everything in the world is a manifestation of consciousness, he or she is simultaneously making a statement about the nature of human consciousness (psychology), declaring a metaphysical position on reality (philosophy), and alluding to the ultimate nature of God (religion). Just as the facets of a diamond reflect different aspects of its surroundings, psychology, philosophy, and religion each reflect a different aspect of the same understanding of the human personality and the basic reality of the universe.

Of course, Western psychology also expresses positions on each of these disciplines when making statements about the world. For instance, when a Western behavioral scientist says that consciousness is nothing more than electrical activity in the brain, she or he is taking a position on psychological and philosophical issues and may be obliquely suggesting a religious position on the nature of God.

Western culture, however, for the past four hundred years, has separated these disciplines and allowed each to pursue its own goals with its own methods. The different cultural norms for intellectual inquiry in the East and West provide advantages and disadvantages for each culture. Often, they can provide a source for misunderstanding as well. For instance, the fact that psychology and religion are not completely separated in the East has been seen as evidence that Eastern perspectives are based on outdated and immature intellectual systems. Of course, it would be just as easy to see Eastern perspectives as examples of interdisciplinary approaches or holistic theories that are, therefore, quite contemporary.

Having stated that the Eastern systems tend to view psychology, philosophy, and religion as intertwined, it is also true that separate systems of psychology, philosophy, and religion have evolved out of this mix. As practitioners of spiritual disciplines like meditation and yoga tried to explain their insights into the human personality and the nature of reality, they used a number of different theoretical and philosophical systems. For instance, Rajmani Tigunait has described seven major schools of philosophy that exist today in Hinduism.[6] Similarly, various Buddhist ideas can be found within a number of different philosophical systems.

As Eastern systems tend to view philosophy, psychology, and theology in ways that are holistic and integrated, the words used to describe those systems in the West can also be somewhat problematic. The title of this book is a perfect example. Referring to these systems as a "psychology" could be as misleading as referring to them as "religion." In fact, the word "psychology" is derived from the ancient Greek and refers roughly to the study of the psyche, or "soul."[7] The Christian idea of a soul is not part of most Eastern systems. Of course, the study of the soul is not part of contemporary Western psychology, either! Nonetheless, a better title for the book may have been *Eastern Wisdom.*[8] Although potentially confusing for many Western readers, it would have captured the holistic element of the Eastern systems.

DEFINITIONS OF WELL-BEING

The second major contrast between Eastern and Western psychologies concerns perspectives, assumptions, and theories of well-being and mental health. Even after a cursory examination of both Western and Eastern personality theories, it becomes apparent that each attempts to describe quite different models of well-being.

Concerning theories of mental health, Western theories tend to focus on adequate adjustment to normal, everyday social realities and the unfortunate consequences of unhealthy personality development or inadequate coping strategies. Western psychology is designed to explore the prediction and control of thoughts, feelings, and behaviors. When interventions are seen as necessary in order to inspire changes, the change techniques are applied directly to troublesome thoughts, emotions, or behaviors. In fact, schools of psychotherapy have evolved that specialize in each of these areas: behaviorism on overt behaviors, cognitive therapy on thoughts, and humanistic styles of therapy on emotions. A major goal is the creation of a resilient and adaptable sense of self-identity that allows a reasonable adjustment to society.

In contrast, Eastern theories focus on optimal adult personality development. The orientation is similar to recent developments in positive psychology that focus on flourishing and the nature of the good life.[9] However, unlike positive psychology—and western psychology in general—the perspectives from Eastern psychology work toward optimal personality development and well-being by fostering certain emotional and behavioral changes rooted in how people perceive the fundamental nature of self-identity and reality. Specifically, Eastern models of mental health place less emphasis on the creation and maintenance of a stable sense of self-identity as it is normally understood. In addition,

Eastern psychologies often focus on alterations in consciousness as the key to changing thoughts, emotions, and behaviors. That is, Eastern psychologies tend to change consciousness so that the psychological context in which emotions and thoughts function can be altered. For instance, meditation practice can help people become more aware of their angry and resentful emotions while simultaneously giving them the ability to no longer identify with or act on those emotions. One of the consequences is that the person remains self-aware, but those troubling emotions lose any power to motivate behavior or to capture thinking in endless ruminations. Further, most of the ideas on well-being in Eastern psychology are tied to spiritual experiences and perspectives.

In general, Western theories of well-being have not focused on spiritual development. In fact, in the past, many Western psychologists and psychiatrists classified dramatic spiritual experiences as either neurotic defenses against anxiety or as pathological. Luckily, that situation is rapidly changing. On the other hand, Eastern theories have not focused on either the determinants of normal social adjustment or on serious psychopathology. Instead, they often view our normal waking consciousness—even in its most mature and rational forms—as immature and as the source of unhappiness. Further explorations into the Eastern perspective on mental health will be covered in chapter 2.

Finally, Eastern psychology postulates developmental stages of optimal well-being that are often defined by altered states of consciousness. Most of these stages are seen as "higher" stages. That is, most are seen as ways of thinking, feeling, and being in the world that are more developmentally advanced than the traditional developmental stage theories of Western personality theory.[10] In fact, Eastern psychologies list numerous states of consciousness that are not recognized by Western psychology. Again, the Eastern perspectives focus on those aspects of altered states of consciousness that are relevant to optimizing psychological well-being, mental health, and personal growth.

DEFINITIONS OF CONSCIOUSNESS

The third major difference between Eastern and Western approaches to psychology concerns ideas about consciousness, especially the ways in which consciousness is approached in the two systems. The close association between states of consciousness and Eastern psychology presents a number of hurdles for people trained in the Western intellectual tradition. First, the idea of consciousness has been an extremely slippery concept in Western psychology and philosophy. In fact, there is no widely accepted definition for consciousness in Western psychology.[11] A short list of the definitions used by Western psychologists would include the following: awareness, intentionality, normal wakeful cognitive activity, the sense of identity or personal unity, and a variety of perspectives that focus on both the process of consciousness and the contents of awareness. So although the problem of consciousness may be *the* central issue for western psychology, because our entire psychological life is situated in conscious experience, an adequate definition of *consciousness* has eluded researchers for years.[12] When the question turns to states of consciousness, Western scientists have generally recognized only three major states of consciousness: waking, sleep, and dreaming—although some argue that hypnosis is a fourth state of consciousness.

Definitions of consciousness also show considerable variation in Eastern psychologies. The most metaphysical concepts generally equate consciousness with all of existence. From this perspective, everything exists in consciousness; consciousness is the substratum of existence—it is not derivative. At other times, consciousness is described as a series of momentary mental states, each of which is ephemeral.[13] As will be discussed next, the term *consciousness* is also applied to different states of consciousness.

Altered States of Consciousness   As Eastern psychologies define a number of alternate states of consciousness, the next logical step is to define what types of alternate states of consciousness are being referred to. As might be expected, the term *"altered state of consciousness"* is quite vague and vulnerable to wildly divergent application. Generally, definitions of alternate states of consciousness are based on the normal wakeful activity model of consciousness. Under most circumstances, people do not notice their consciousness—it is simply present. Certainly, most people fail to recognize that normal waking consciousness is a holistic construction formed from an integration of inputs from physiological, perceptual, emotional, and cognitive domains. In the West, conscious attempts to induce or cultivate altered states are often seen as either self-indulgent escapes from reality or dissociative states that may be symptoms of mental illness. Certainly, any insights that people claim to have found while in those states are viewed with extreme skepticism.

It should be understood that in Eastern theories of personality and mental health, not all alternate states are of interest and not all insights are accepted as valid. In general, changes that are of interest are alterations in specific emotional experiences, the sense of meaningfulness, and especially in the sense of self and identity. Alterations of consciousness that are induced for recreational purposes are usually not of interest. On the other hand, changes in sense of meaning—such as those found in a profound mystical experience—are of great interest. After all, Eastern cultures have known about naturally occurring psychedelic and other psychotropic drugs for many years. Yet, the practitioners generally do not use drugs to induce spiritual experiences, instead focusing on meditation and other spiritual practices.

Charles Tart has done considerable work on alternate states of consciousness from the perspective of Western psychology. He defined a discrete altered state of consciousness (d-ASC) as follows:

> ...a *radical* alteration of the overall patterning of consciousness... such that the experiencer of the d-ASC (or perhaps an observer) can tell that different laws are functioning, that a new, overall pattern is superimposed on his experience...[the] radical changes in the parts that constitute the pattern may include major quantitative shifts in the range of functioning of psychological and/or physiological functions such as memory, reasoning, sense of identity, and motor skills, and the temporary disappearance of some functions and the emergence of new functions not available in ordinary consciousness.[14]

This definition does suggest some of the major issues. As defined in Eastern psychology, an alternate state of consciousness is a significant or *radical* shift in perception, cognitive ability, mood, or meaning system. Further, the shift must be significantly different, either qualitatively, quantitatively, or both, from changes in functioning that occur as part of normal everyday experience. Finally, different rules of psychological functioning must appear to be operating. Seen from this definition, being in an especially good mood on one day is not an alternate state of consciousness, while experiencing a profound religious epiphany about the nature of God is most likely an alternate state.

Eastern perspectives also postulate a far greater number of alternate states of consciousness than are found in Western psychology. As stated above, Western psychology recognizes only three major states of consciousness. Although this statement is essentially true, it tends to obscure the fact that Western psychology also recognizes variations in consciousness such as exercise-induced mood enhancements, flow, burst of creativity, peak experiences, intoxication, religious conversion experiences, and even intense states of romantic love. Eastern psychological systems, however, provide a systematic classification of a wide variety of alternate states that are not recognized by Western psychology. For example, the Vedic psychology of Hinduism postulates seven major states of consciousness.[15] Three of these are the familiar waking, sleep, and dreaming. The other four are not found in western psychology: transcendent, cosmic, refined cosmic, and unity consciousness. Each of these in turn is further subdivided into finer gradations of consciousness. In the Buddhist tradition, one manual describes 121 different conscious states and 52 factors of consciousness.[16]

The famous anthropologist Mircea Eliade wrote about what he termed "technologies of the sacred."[17] These appeared in societies that developed a number of practical methods for the induction of altered states, as well as methods to utilize those states for various social or personal goals. Eastern psychologies have discovered very practical methods for the induction of altered states of consciousness that theoretically lead to increased mental health and healthy personality development. The core teachings of Buddhism, Hinduism, and Taoism contain the results of personal experiments with altered states conducted over literally thousands of years. A number of those techniques will be covered later, in chapter 4.

MYSTICISM AND RELIGIOUS EXPERIENCES

The fourth contrast between Eastern and Western psychology centers on the place of mysticism in psychological investigations of consciousness. As stated previously, Eastern psychologies are primarily based in the contemplative religious and spiritual traditions. The term *contemplative spirituality* is used to describe religious disciplines that seek to find a direct and very personal experience of God.[18] That is, they are founded upon practices that are designed to produce personal and emotional religious experiences that are psychologically transforming for the person and allow for the creation of deeper—usually spiritual—meaning systems. Specifically, Eastern psychologies are derived from a type of religious practice known as *mysticism*.

The term refers to any practice that seeks a direct and personal experience of God, Spirit, Atman, Buddha Nature, or whatever is taken to be of Ultimate Concern.[19] The core definitional postulate of mysticism is that it is possible for individuals to experience a transcendent spiritual reality. Having a spiritual experience such as this is said to be an extremely positive emotional experience and can result in a spiritual transformation or spiritual conversion.[20] This mystical experience is usually very emotional, frequently psychologically transformative, and should also lead to behavior changes. The descriptors used in Eastern psychology for these experiences vary by culture and by situation, but the most familiar terms in the West are *enlightenment* and *nirvana* (*nibbana*, P). Since Zen Buddhism is so popular in the West, another term often seen is *satori* (*sah-TOR-ee*), which usually refers to a single enlightenment experience. While most Western psychologists know very little about mystical experiences, the study of mysticism is, in fact, a recognized specialty of some Western psychologists.[21]

William James, who is often described as the father of American psychology, was one of the first Western psychologists to be interested in mystical and religious experiences. James believed that mystical experiences were marked by two distinctive characteristics. The first was *ineffability*, or the difficulty people encounter when trying to adequately describe the experience in words. Indeed, many people say that language is a completely inadequate tool for conveying the experience to others. The second of James's characteristics was that mystical experiences had a *noetic* quality. This referred to the fact that many mystical experiences bring with them a deep sense that some absolutely fundamental knowledge, a profound insight into the nature of the world, has been revealed in the experience.

Eva Wong has presented four basic components of mysticism.[22] The first is a *cognitive* component. This is the experience of an underlying unity behind the apparent diversity in the world. It is assumed that this unity cannot be understood with ordinary perceptual or rational means. The second is an *emotional* component, concerned with states of ecstasy, joy, and bliss. The third is a *perceptual* component. Here, the focus is on heightened awareness and the alternate states of consciousness that are often part of mystical experiences. Finally, there is a *behavioral* component. This can include either the actions that help induce it, such as meditation or yoga, or the behavior changes that should result from the experience, such as increased humility, altruism, and compassion toward others.

W. T. Stace completed one of the classic studies on mysticism.[23] He compiled a list of seven basic characteristics of the mystical experience by examining reports from every major Eastern and Western religion. Stace said that reports of profound mystical experiences are marked by the following:

(1) The emergence of a unitary, undifferentiated consciousness

(2) A sense that the experience is located in neither time nor space

(3) A feeling that what is experienced represents some ultimate reality

(4) Emotions such as peace, bliss, joy, and ecstasy

(5) A sense that the person has encountered something sacred

(6) Paradoxical violations of the rules of logic

(7) Ineffability, or a feeling that the experience cannot be described in words

Stace further classified mystical experiences into two types. *Introvertive* mystical experiences involve a sense that the individual self disappears as it merges with, or dissolves into, a unitary consciousness beyond space or time and without form or content. *Extrovertive* mystical experiences involve an experience in which the self has reached a unity with the multiplicity and diversity of the world; the self has become "one" with the universe. Ralph Hood's research has supported a third component: a dimension defined by joyous emotion, awe, wonder, and revelation, all of which the person interprets from a religious or spiritual viewpoint.[24]

Ineffability of Mystical Experiences As mentioned above, one of the major assumptions of mysticism involves the ineffability or inexpressibility of mystical experiences. It is assumed that mystical experiences are impossible to adequately express in common, everyday language. For example, Rajmani Tigunait describes how the Vedanta system of Hinduism conceptualizes the ultimate reality of the universe by saying:

> [T]he highest truth, the absolute; it is beyond all phenomena in existence, beyond time, space, and causation, and it cannot be experienced by the senses or the [normal] mind. The entire phenomenal world is confined by time, space, and causation, and as long as one remains bound by these concepts, his experience is limited. But beyond the realms of time and space, there is an absolute unconditional reality that has no beginning and no end. That is called Atman, the Self.[25]

Since the ultimate reality is beyond all phenomena in existence; beyond time, space, and causation; and cannot be experienced by the senses or the normal mind, it is also impossible to adequately describe the ultimate reality in words. This inexpressible quality is found in the Hindu Upanishads, where it is said that the description of Brahman that is the most free of error is "*neti, neti*", which translates as "neither this, nor that."[26] Paradoxically, the only way to talk about it is to say what it is not. Zen master Yasutani-roshi has said, "Our true nature is beyond all categories. Whatever you can conceive or imagine is but a fragment of your self. Hence, the real you cannot be found through reason, deduction, or intellectual analysis, or even endless imaginings."[27]

Theoretically, certain alternate states of consciousness provide access to modes of perception that allow the limiting categories of language to be transcended. The Taoist Sage Chuang-Tzu said:

> Tao is obscured when men understand only one of a pair of opposites, or concentrate only on a partial aspect of being. Then

clear expression also becomes muddled by mere wordplay.... Better to abandon this hopeless effort and seek true light! [28]

One of the most significant difficulties in understanding Eastern psychology is that it may be necessary to have experienced certain alternate states of consciousness in order to fully understand many statements made by practitioners. Lama Govinda, an Englishman who became a Tibetan monk, expressed the difficulty this way:

> To discuss metaphysical problems on the common plane of consciousness is like discussing sexual problems with children who have not yet attained maturity. Such discussions are not only useless but also harmful. We can only understand of the world as much as we have developed within ourselves. [29] *Lama Govinda*

Of course, in order to understand Western science, it is also necessary to have specific preliminary training. In research psychology, a person needs training in statistics and research design. In physics, knowledge of higher mathematics is necessary in order to fully evaluate the theoretical concepts and findings of those disciplines.

Before leaving the topic of mysticism, it must be said that the mystical element of religion is not confined only to eastern religions. In fact, every major religion of the world has a mystical sect and a body of esoteric teachings that are designed to help devotees experience a perceived union with God or the ultimate reality. [30] In the Western world, the most visible example is the monastic tradition of Catholicism. [31] However, there is also a strong mystical branch of Judaism, [32] as well as the Sufi sect in Islam. [33] In the Western world, most people are unaware of the teachings of, or even the existence of, the mystical branch of their own religion. In contrast, most Hindus, Buddhists, or Taoists are quite aware of the mystical foundations of their faith, even if they personally are not involved in spiritual practices.

THE USE OF INTROSPECTION

The fifth major contrast between Eastern and Western approaches to psychology concerns the methodology used to investigate human behavior and personality. In the Western world, since the nineteenth century, this method has traditionally been scientific research, with its standards of objectivity and measurability. In the East, the method used has primarily been phenomenological investigations or introspection. In fact, the theoretical positions of Eastern psychology are almost entirely derived from introspection and insights acquired during meditation. For example, in the Buddhist tradition, three types of knowledge are described. The first type is opinion, which is not based upon reason but upon personal desires. The second type is knowledge based upon reason and intellectual reflection. This is the type utilized by science. The third type is intuition gained through disciplined meditation. In contrast to the West, this last type of knowledge is seen as superior to the other two.[34]

Western academic and research psychology has distrusted introspection as a method for directly investigating psychological questions almost since psychology first described itself as a science in the late nineteenth century. Ironically, the first laboratory experiments in scientific psychology were based on the use of introspection. However, these early psychologists found that introspection introduced too many problems into their experiments. Indeed, empirical studies have shown that in many instances, people are quite unaware of the factors that influence their thinking, emotional responses, or behavior.[35]

Like Western psychology, meditative disciplines also assume that human perception can be distorted by personal biases and should, therefore, not be taken as a final truth about reality. The meditation disciplines also recognize that not all insights gained in meditation are glimpses of truth. The experiences arrived at during meditation must be validated by highly experienced meditation masters. The fact that false insights can provide traps or dead ends during meditation practice is well known to meditation students. In fact, there is a rich and often amusing literature in Eastern psychology that describes confrontations between novice meditators and meditation masters. In these stories, the novices believe that with their latest meditative insight, they have achieved true enlightenment, or nirvana. However, more often than not, the mediation master dismisses those insights as mere fantasy or illusion, and the student is advised to go deeper with her or his meditations.

HOLISM AND INTERDEPENDENCY

The sixth major contrast between Eastern and Western psychology may seem a bit closer to philosophy than psychology. This contrast concerns how people should explain the workings of the universe. When attempting to explain the nature of the world and how it functions, Western scientific psychology has relied most heavily on reductionism. In reductionism, the world and human beings are understood by reducing the complexity down to what seem to be fundamental elements. After the fundamental elements are delineated—for instance, the basic emotions or the basic traits of personality—then attempts are made to create larger, more complex structures. Usually, the connections among the basic elements are described with simple linear models of causality. For instance, a child's helpful behavior is seen as an attempt to gain positive rewards, or a fear of adult success is seen as being caused by old, unconscious fears of a domineering and punishing father.

In Eastern psychology, as each person is innately connected to an underlying reality, it follows that each action in life can have consequences that reverberate throughout all existence. In the *Diamond Sutra* of Buddhism, the metaphor for this interconnectedness is Indra's Net. This image is of a vast necklace of diamonds, where each facet of each diamond reflects the other facets in an infinite variety. Moreover, change is not predetermined. At any point in time, a number of possible events could occur, depending upon the dynamic relationships among past, present, and future. In Hinduism, this dynamic interconnectedness of all life is thought to have a playful quality. It is referred to as *lila,* or the divine cosmic dance of the universe.

Ted Kaptchuk suggests the differences between the Taoist and Western perspectives in his description of Chinese medicine. He says that Western medicine is based on the idea that for each unique disease, a specific cause must be found. In Chinese medicine, however, the physician looks for a "pattern of disharmony" rather than a specific cause. In fact, the idea of causation that exists in Western scientific thought is almost entirely absent from Chinese medicine. In Chinese thought, any specific cause is secondary to an overall pattern created from the relationships among all of the patient's symptoms and how they exist in the context of that patient's life. In the Chinese system, "events unfold

TCM - looks for the pattern of disharmony

through a kind of spontaneous cooperation, an inner dynamic in the nature of things...the universe is continuously changing. Its movement is the result not of a first cause or creator, but of an inner dynamic of cyclical patterns."[36] Therefore, no disease can be understood without taking into account the web of physiological, social, and psychological relationships that are present for a unique patient at that particular point in time. Kaptchuk says that because it is the pattern that is important, two patients who have identical symptoms from a Western standpoint might be diagnosed with two different conditions by a Chinese physician and treated in two different ways, because their web of relationships are different. Kaptchuk quotes Joseph Needleman, who described the Chinese view of causation by saying, "Things influence one another not by acts of mechanistic causation, but by a kind of 'inductance'...the key word in Chinese thought is *order* and above all *pattern*...."[37]

In Eastern thought, consciousness is studied as a dynamic and holistic phenomenon related to the web of factors and relationships in a person's life—or even past lives. Lynne Hagen has described this perspective by saying, "The universe is a symbiosis of all that exists. When a particular part of the universe is analyzed, classified, and compartmentalized, conflict arises and the larger pattern and meaning within the universe is lost."[38] Nevertheless, as we will see later, Eastern psychologies can be very analytical in their descriptions of types of consciousness.

Thinking about Time   Most Eastern psychologies are also based on the idea of a universe that exists outside of time. Most Eastern religious and philosophical positions assume that the world had no beginning and will have no end; the universe evolves through endless cycles rather than through linear time. There is also no creation myth based on the idea that the word came into being at a single moment in time. While Hinduism does have a myth that describes cycles of creation and destruction of the universe, in the myth, these cycles have no beginning and no end.[39]

THE VARIETIES OF EASTERN PSYCHOLOGY

At this point, it will be helpful to provide a very brief historical overview of Hinduism, Buddhism, and Taoism. Hopefully, this will provide a bit more context for the Eastern perspective on psychology. It should be noted that since some Eastern religions have a 5,000 year history, the number of sects found in the world today is quite extensive. Therefore, what will be presented here are the major sects that are active today and that have the most impact on an Eastern approach to psychology.

HINDUISM AND YOGA

Hinduism, found today primarily in India, is the oldest living religious tradition in the world.[40] Hinduism is a remarkably complex amalgam of different perspectives. Some have suggested that Hinduism should not be considered a single religion, but rather a collection of religious orientations.[41]

The civilization that gave rise to Hinduism was prospering by at least 3,000 BCE. The oldest known sacred texts of Hinduism are collectively known as the *Vedas*. The Vedas may have been transmitted orally for at least 1,000 years before the earliest book, the Rig-Veda, was written down, beginning about 1,400 BCE (although some portions may be as old as 1,900 BCE). The books of the Veda contain sacred songs, chants (or *mantras*), prayers to deities, philosophical ideas, and instructions for the practice of various rituals. Rajmani Tigunait describes the *Rig-Veda* (or Rg Veda) by saying:

> The *Rig Veda* is a collection of poetic hymns in which numerous gods and goddesses—who are personifications of different aspects of the forces of nature—are invoked and glorified. The hymns appear to be simple prayers to the deities. Yet, couched in highly symbolic language, they contain great philosophical and metaphysical meaning.[42]

The last section of the Vedas contains the Upanishads, which were composed around 800 BCE.[43] This section focuses attention on two questions: what is the nature of the human self and what is the nature of reality.

The best-known sacred text in Hinduism is the *Bhagavad-Gita*, which was composed between 400 BCE and 100 BCE.[44] The story contained in the Bhagavad-Gita seems an odd choice for a religious text. The story is set on a battlefield, as two armies are about to go to war. In the story, two principle characters, Arjuna and the god Krishna, discuss a number of conflicts and doubts that Arjuna struggles with before the battle. The setting, however, is symbolic. Mark Muesse explains that "the battlefield is really a metaphor for the soul, the self, the mind, and its struggle... [It is] a metaphor for the self and its internal struggles."[45] A number of the classic teachings of yoga are contained in the Bhagavad-Gita.

The reference to metaphor and symbolic language in the Vedas is very important to understanding Hinduism. Throughout the sacred literature of Hinduism, one reads of various gods and goddesses engaged in political intrigue, love trysts, or military battles. However, each of these stories is meant to be interpreted symbolically rather than literally. The gods and goddesses of Hinduism represent personifications of forces of nature and aspects of human psychology.

Yoga Any discussion of Eastern psychology must give a prominent place to the discipline and philosophical system called yoga. The word *yoga* is derived from a term that means "to yoke together," or to unite. As Huston Smith put it, the purpose of yoga is to integrate or "unite the human spirit with the God who lies concealed in its deepest recesses."[46] The classic text that is relevant to the current discussion is the *Yoga Sutras*. The sage who collected these sutras, or instruction manuals, was named Patanjali. Historians know virtually nothing about his life. For instance, estimates of when he lived vary from 4,000 BCE to about 500 CE; the exact date is unknown.[47] His system describes many aspects of the human personality and gives instructions for using yoga to help people access a transcendent reality and find liberation from suffering. Yoga recognizes that people approach life in different ways, and there needs to be a number of avenues open to people as they pursue spiritual practices. Therefore, eight types of yoga are practiced today as a way to match personality types with the most compatible spiritual practices.

Types of Yoga *Hatha* yoga, or the yoga of the body, is probably the most familiar to Westerners. This discipline focuses on physical postures that help purify and strengthen the body. *Karma* yoga, or the yoga of action, focuses on service to others and compassion. *Jnana* yoga, or the yoga of knowledge, is the practice of rigorous self-analysis and philosophy. For people who are emotionally inclined, there is *Bhakiti* yoga, or the yoga of devotion, where the focus is on intense devotion and love. *Mantra* yoga, or the yoga of sound, uses the repetition of sacred sounds to increase concentration during meditation. The yoga of sitting meditation is *Laya* yoga. One of the more esoteric to Westerners is *Kundalini* yoga, or the yoga of energy. This style uses postures, visualizations, and meditation to raise energy through energy channels of the body that are postulated in Hindu psychology (see "Tantra" below). Finally, the practice of *Raja* yoga, or the "royal road," tends to focus on psychological and physical control. This is the yoga of Patanjali and is seen by some as a combination of the other styles of yoga. It is also known as the most psychological of the yoga styles. In this book, the emphasis will be on *Raja* yoga.

Tantra   The ideas of tantra evolved around 500 CE. One of the major thrusts of tantra was to provide techniques to help people achieve enlightenment without separating spirit and embodiment. The Vedantic writings of Hinduism often viewed the body as unclean and a hindrance to spiritual awakening. Spiritual techniques focused on releasing the spiritual self from the "chains" of the body (note the similarity to Christian ideas about the battle between flesh and spirit). In contrast, tantra saw the body as a vehicle for manifesting the subtle energies and using them for spiritual purposes. The release of this energy can be very dramatic, and most consider these practices to be dangerous without a competent teacher or guru. Georg Feuerstein has referred to tantra as an "integrative" approach, where the body is a platform or foundation for realizing spiritual liberation. The older approach, which emphasizes higher states of consciousness that transcend an impure body, he calls "verticalist" approaches.[48] Tantra has also been known in the West because of its association with certain sexual techniques designed to raise kundalini energy (see chapter 4).

BUDDHISM

Buddhism began with the teachings of one person who lived in northern India from about 560 to 480 BCE.[49] In his earlier life, his name was Siddhartha Gautama, but after his final enlightenment he became the

Buddha, or "The Awakened One." The Buddha taught a method to help liberate people from suffering and unhappiness. From his spiritual awakening around the age of thirty until his death at age eighty, he was a wandering monk who taught a very practical method for achieving lasting happiness and peace of mind. Buddhism is found today primarily in Nepal, Southeast Asia, the Tibetan plateau, Japan, and Korea. It is also one of the fastest-growing religious perspectives in the Western world. Some sects of Buddhism tend to place less emphasis on dramatic, altered states of consciousness and more emphasis on living in the moment. In the world today, there are three major schools of Buddhism, described below.

Theravada Buddhism Within the first one hundred years after the death of the Buddha, a number of Buddhist sects developed. One of the earliest sects that survives today is called Theravada ("the way of the elders"). In the past, many believed that the teachings of the Theravada school were the closest to the original teachings of the Buddha. However, recent scholarship suggests that the very early history of Buddhism is quite complex, and it is difficult to assign "original" status to any one school of thought.[50] In Theravada, the ideal for human personality development is the *arhat*, or someone who has achieved the highest level of spiritual development. An arhat will enter final nirvana and will be released from further rebirths upon his or her death.

The written records of the Buddha's teachings are collectively known as the Pali Canon, named after the Pali language of Sri Lanka, the country in which Buddhist monks finally wrote down the teachings in use today. The Pali Canon has three parts, known as the Tripitaka ("Three Baskets"). Contained in the Pali Canon is a section titled the *Abhidharma-pitaka* ("Basket of Special Learning"). This last section, in particular, contains the core teachings of Buddhist psychology.

Mahayana Buddhism The other important Buddhist sect that survives today is the Mahayana ("the great vehicle"). Mahayana began to develop around the first century BCE and focused on a practice style that was open to lay practitioners and not just monks and nuns. The ideal of human personality development was the *bodhisattva*. Like the arhat, the bodhisattva was a person who had achieved the highest level of spiritual development and could enter final nirvana and thus be released from further reincarnations in the world. Instead, the bodhisattva vows to remain in this world and help everyone else enter nirvana first. Mahayana practice styles also tended to be more elaborate than Theravada styles in terms of cosmology, iconography, and ritual.

As there are also some philosophical and metaphysical differences from Theravada, the Mahayana school developed their own set of scriptures in addition to the Pali Canon. These include a number of *sutras* (teachings of the Buddha), *shastras* (elaborations of points of doctrine), and *tantras* (texts on esoteric teachings and practices). Among the more central texts of Mahayana Buddhism are the Lotus, the Diamond, and the Heart Sutras.

Ch'an and Zen While the Theravada school spread to Sri Lanka and then to Southeast Asia, Mahayana spread north into China and Tibet. When Buddhism moved into China, it adopted many of the nature-oriented ideas of Taoism and developed a style of meditation practice known as Ch'an.[51] The Ch'an style spread to Korea and Japan between 600 and 800 CE and became Zen. The Zen practice style focuses on naturalness, spontaneity, and sitting meditation. It seeks immediate, direct insight over an intellectual understanding of Buddhism. Two major schools of Zen have had the most influence in the West: Soto and Rinzai. Zen master Dogen Zenji created the Soto school in the thirteenth century. In the Soto school, meditation practice centers on shikan-taza, or "just sitting." This practice focuses on a profound awareness of the present moment without any special technique or method of meditation. Therefore, Soto practice tends to deemphasize seeking enlightenment experiences as a future goal for one's meditation, focusing instead on awareness of each moment. Rinzai was created by the Chinese master Li-chin I-hsan in the ninth century and was introduced to Japan by master Eisai in the twelfth century. In the Rinzai school, practitioners are often confronted with, or confounded by, a number of sometimes dramatic techniques designed to break through the grip that our ordinary minds use to give our sense of self a feeling of permanent reality. Rinzai practice tends to focus on enlightenment experiences, at least as an initial goal of spiritual practice.

Elements of Zen became extremely important in Japanese culture. The influence of Zen is especially seen in the arts, where all the arts— and even the simple act of serving tea—have been profoundly influenced by Zen philosophy and practices.[52]

Vajrayana Buddhism When Buddhism spread to Tibet in about the ninth century CE, the result was a style that focused on a more direct, immediate access to enlightened consciousness. It was called Vajrayana, or the Diamond Vehicle, in reference to the purity of its teachings. Tibetan Buddhism borrowed more heavily from yoga and tantra than other branches of Buddhism. In fact, some have referred to Vajrayana as "tantric Buddhism." It also created a complex cosmology filled with gods, bodhisattvas, and other celestial beings. As in Hinduism, all of these are personifications of aspects of the human personality.

Schools of Vajrayana Buddhism Within the Vajrayana tradition today, there are four major schools.[53] The *Nyingma* school traces its teaching back to the Indian sage Padmasambhava, who is one of the founders of Tibetan Buddhism. This school focuses on a set of meditation practices known as dzogchen, which focus on emptiness. The *Sakya* school tends to focus on scholastic practices. The *Kagyu* school is associated with three important mediation masters: Milarepa, Naropa, and Marpa. The Kagyu school practices the mahamudra style of meditation that begins with one-pointed concentration and leads to a transcendence of all intellectual concepts. Finally, the *Geluk* school places emphasis on the cultivation of compassion and the realization of emptiness. The Dalai Lama has always come from this school.

The Tibetan Buddhist canon, or standard collection of sacred texts, was compiled around the fourteenth century, although modifications to the standard collection are common. The texts that comprise the canon are divided into the *Kahgyur*, which is said to be the words of the Buddha, and the *Tengyur*, which is a collection of commentaries and other texts from a variety of Buddhist sources. In all, the canon consists of about 224 volumes.

TAOISM

Taoist beliefs may have existed in China in a nascent form as early as 4,000 BCE. The fundamental beliefs of Taoism, however, began to coalesce in China around 700 BCE. The person usually cited as the founder of Taoism is Lao-tzu. Despite his prominence in Taoism, historians know next to nothing about him, or even if he was a real person. Lao-tzu is listed as the author of the *Tao Te Ching, or The Way and Its Power*, which is the most famous text of Taoism. However, scholars agree that the book certainly had multiple authors who lived over a period of several hundred years.[54]

Taoism is based on the idea of the *Tao,* or the "impersonal and unnamable force behind the workings of the universe."[55] It is the supreme principle of order, or the reality behind the origin of the universe; it is the life principle. Huston Smith addresses another quality: "Although the Tao is transcendent, it is also immanent...it is the way of the universe, the norm, the rhythm, the driving power in all nature, the ordering principle behind all life."[56] In the language of ancient China, the root meaning of Tao is "path" or "way." When used as a verb, Tao means "to guide" or "to direct."

In addition to the *Tao Te Ching,* the second most important work of Taoism is the *Chuang-tzu,* which was written around the fourth century BCE by Chuang-tzu (or Chuang Chou), along with some of his students.[57] The third major text of Taoism, which also dates from about the fourth century BCE, is the *Lieh-tzu,* which was written by Lieh Yu-k'ou. The oldest work that contains Taoist ideas is the *I Ching, or The Book of Changes.* The oral tradition that eventually became this book may have begun around 4,000 BCE. On the surface, this text appears to be simply a book on divination. However, many of the principles of Taoism can be found in this text. There is also a Taoist Canon, or collection of the central texts of Taoism. The canon is referred to as the *Tao Tsang,* and it contains around 1,400 titles divided into three major sections. This compilation was completed in the fifteenth and sixteenth centuries.

Major Schools of Taoism Over the years, Taoism developed a number of divisions and sects that emphasized different aspects of Taoist practices.[58] In *magical Taoism*, or the way of power, the goal is to harness the forces in the universe and use them for spiritual or humanitarian purposes. In *divinational Taoism*, or the way of seeing, the goal is to see the patterns of change in the universe. It attempts to see the movement of Tao in all things and to appreciate how the flux and interdependency of all things creates a pattern of change. The art of *feng-shui, or of designing* buildings to enhance the positive energies of the universe, comes from divinational Taoism. In feng-shui, the land is alive and filled with energy, so buildings must be designed to take advantage of those energies. The ancient Chinese book of divination, the *I Ching*, also comes out of this school. *Ceremonial Taoism* is the way of devotion. It is concerned with performance of ceremonies and rituals that will influence deities and powers of nature, as well as renew and strengthen the bond between humans and deities. *Action and Karma Taoism* is the way of right action. In this school, good deeds or thoughts bring rewards, and wrong deeds bring retribution. Deities such as the Jade Emperor are responsible for tallying one's deeds, and the actions of each generation affect future generations. *Internal-alchemical Taoism*, or the way of inner transformation, is the primary source for ideas about psychological transformation. In this book, most references to Taoism will be references to the internal-alchemical school, or the way of inner transformation.

CLOSING THOUGHTS

This first chapter began by briefly summarizing a few of the major differences between an Eastern approach to psychology and the traditional Western approach. In general, Eastern psychologies affirm spiritual transformation as the path to genuine and lasting mental health; they value disciplined, controlled introspection as a valid method of investigation and view consciousness as more primary than physical matter. In this way, they see the physical materialism, detached objectivity, and strict linguistic categorization of modern science as a very limited approach to the pursuit of well-being. Interestingly, both Eastern and Western approaches value and use rules of formal logic and analysis, both search for valid and reliable truths, and both look for methods that can be generalized and applied to help people achieve better lives. The

Dalai Lama's words opened this chapter, and now I would like to close with his comments on science and introspective methods.

> The study of consciousness...has two components. One is what happens to the brain and to the behavior of the individual (what brain science and behavior psychology are equipped to explore), but the other is the phenomenological experience of the cognitive, emotional, and psychological states themselves. It is for this latter element that the application of a first-person [introspective] method is essential. To put it another way, although the experience of happiness may coincide with certain chemical reactions in the brain... no amount of biochemical and neurological description of this brain change can explain what happiness is.[59]

CHAPTER 2

Well-being in Eastern Psychology

One day as the Buddha was meditating, a man named Dona approached him. Dona was struck by the serenity and tranquility expressed by the Buddha and questioned him.

Dona:	Are you, by chance, a saint?
The Buddha:	No.
Dona:	Are you an angel or spirit?
The Buddha:	No.
Dona:	Are you a god?
The Buddha:	No.
Dona:	Then, what are you?
The Buddha:	I am awake.

FROM THE DONA-SUTRA

To understand the perspective of Eastern psychology, it is essential to understand the unique approach to well-being and mental health that forms its core. All aspects of the Eastern approach to psychology are in the service of a specific definition of optimal well-being and all knowledge about psychological processes should be utilized to help people overcome the causes of human unhappiness. The analysis of what causes that unhappiness, however, reaches conclusions and recommendations for interventions that differ significantly from efforts of Western psychologists to solve similar problems.

The theories of well-being and mental health expressed in Eastern psychology are all grounded in fundamental metaphysical assumptions about the nature of reality. In fact, since these ideas express positions on the ultimate nature of reality, and therefore may suggest positions on the nature of God, these ideas are the primary source of the religious elements of Eastern psychology. To understand many aspects of Eastern psychology, it is necessary to be familiar with these assumptions. It is not necessary, however, to accept these assumptions to use the ideas and techniques of Eastern psychology. That is, a person can practice yoga, meditation, tai chi chuan, or other martial arts without having to accept these assumptions.

BASIC METAPHYSICAL ASSUMPTIONS

When discussing metaphysical assumptions, we are referring to ideas about the ultimate nature of the universe or assumptions about the inherent nature of reality. Although each system differs somewhat, in general most perspectives in Eastern psychology include the idea that behind or beneath all the various material manifestations of the world, there exists an ultimate ground of existence that embodies the final reality and an ultimate truth of the universe. This ultimate ground is nonmaterial, limitless, infinite, and the source of all the manifestations of the visible universe.

WORLDVIEW OF HINDUISM

In the Vedanta philosophy of Hinduism, this fundamental reality has three basic attributes: it is pure being, pure consciousness, and pure bliss. The word given to this underlying essential reality is *Brahman* (BRA-mahn). This is also the source of what is called the cosmic Self (the capital "S" is deliberately used to distinguish this term from the individual self associated with a sense of personal identity). According to Vedanta philosophy, each individual is Brahman, the universal consciousness. The unique expression in each individual is termed the *Atman* (AHT-man), the god within, or the transcendental Self, which is "considered to be omniscient, omnipotent, and omnipresent...the perfect state of perfect bliss, beauty, and consciousness."[60] The renowned comparative theologian Huston Smith describes this basic assumption of Hinduism as follows:

> Underlying the human self, and animating it, is a reservoir of being that never dies, is never exhausted, and is unrestricted in consciousness. This infinite center of every life, this hidden self or Atman, is no less than Brahman, the Godhead...
>
> Hinduism sees the mind's hidden continents stretching to infinity. Infinite in being, infinite in awareness, there is nothing beyond them that remains unknown. Infinite in joy, too, for there is nothing alien to them to mar their beatitude.[61]

In Hinduism, the underlying essence or fundamental reality is often described with words such as "pure awareness," "consciousness," or "being," giving this foundational reality a living, human presence—for these are qualities of human experience. Unfortunately, for most people, this underlying spiritual essence is buried so deeply beneath the weight of common everyday concerns, worries, and goal pursuits that it is completely hidden from conscious awareness.

WORLDVIEW OF BUDDHISM

The most profound teaching of Hinduism, Vedanta, predates and agrees with many Buddhist ideas. However, in Buddhism, there is no concept of either an ultimate Self or an enduring soul. Buddhism emphasized that the spiritual ground of existence is beyond any possible ideas, conceptualizations, or verbal descriptions. In Mahayana Buddhism, the term often used to describe the ultimate nature of the universe is *sunyata* (soon-YAH-*tah*), the Void, or emptiness. Emptiness refers to the absence of phenomenal existence. The intention of the concept is to emphasize the complete inexpressibility of any idea about ultimate reality. It is assumed that the fundamental reality of the universe is inexpressible in words. The ultimate reality transcends all conceptual dualities, even the fundamental duality expressed by "it is" and "it is not."[62] Buddhist scholar T. V. R. Murti has said that the concept of sunyata is the central, pivotal concept of Buddhism—especially of Mahayana Buddhism.[63]

Buddhists often use another term to speak of ultimate reality—they often use the term *dharma* (DAR=*ma*). Somewhat confusingly, the word dharma can have multiple meanings in Buddhism, ranging from the teachings of the Buddha to the ultimate reality. Early Buddhism also distinguished itself from Hinduism by proclaiming the truth of *anatta* (ah-NAH-tah), or the doctrine of no soul.[64] Anatta refers to the idea that there is no permanent self, either the conventional idea of self-identity or a Transcendent Self.

WORLDVIEW OF TAOISM

In Taoism is found a term that expresses the ultimate reality, the ultimate ground, or the fundamental force that animates and guides the universe. The *Tao* is the name given to this fundamental reality. Taoist scholar Eva Wong describes the Tao in the following way:

> The Tao is the source of all things. It is nameless, invisible, and ungraspable by normal modes of perception. It is bound-less and cannot be exhausted, although all things depend on it for existence. Hidden beneath transition and change, the Tao is the permanent underlying reality...the sky, the earth, rivers, and mountains are part of a larger and unified power, known as Tao, which is an impersonal and unnamed force behind the working of the universe.[65]

Wong goes on to explain that although the Tao is not viewed as a type of spirit or deity, in the early years of Taoism, it was seen as having a benevolent, even a feminine, quality to it. Later, the Tao was seen as a more neutral force of the universe. Although the Tao still possessed its other qualities, it simply did not have any particular benevolent intentionality toward humanity.

Taoism also has a concept that appears remarkably similar to emptiness. The void is *wu* (woo), the mystical "womb" associated with emptiness. Metaphorically, it is like a wheel hub, a clay pot, or a valley because it is efficacious by allowing other things to come into being. Somewhat paradoxically, a person who is empty or purified of all passion and desire can then be fully inhabited by the Tao. The *Tao te Ching* says:

> We join spokes together in a wheel,
> but it is the center hole
> that makes the wagon move.
>
> We shape clay into a pot,
> but it is the emptiness inside
> that holds whatever we want.
>
> We hammer wood for a house,
> but it is the inner space
> that makes it livable.
>
> We work with being,
> but non-being is what we use.[66]

IMAGES AND METAPHORS FOR REALITY

In the East, there are any number of metaphors or images that have been used to describe how each person is connected to a vast universal force or consciousness. One image is of a vast tree, where each leaf that emerges from the tree is a new human consciousness. Each leaf emerges from the universe and is separate, yet connected, to the larger reality. In the Buddhist tradition, it is common to find the image of a vast lake, with numerous small waves being created by the wind. Like the image of the leaf, this image demonstrates how each wave can have an individual existence but is fundamentally connected to the lake, as well as to all the other waves on the lake. To continue the analogy a bit further, when each wave is created, it emerges from the lake to become a separate expression of the lake; and when it disappears, it merges back into the lake or universe as a whole. The *Tao te Ching* says:

Tao is empty—
　　Its use never exhausted.
Bottomless—
　　The origin of all things.
It blunts sharp edges,
　　Unites knots,
　　Softens glare,
　　Becomes one with the dusty world.
Deeply subsistent—
I don't know whose child it is.
It is older than the Ancestor.[67]

One of the most familiar symbols from Eastern psychology is the t'ai-chi symbol from Taoism (figure 2.1). Eva Wong notes that the modern symbol is a combination of two older ones: the Wu-chi Diagram (i.e., a circle) and the t'ai-chi, or Great Ultimate (i.e., a symbol of interacting opposite colors).[68] Wu-chi is the Tao, or the state of stillness and the origin of all things, whereas t'ai-chi is the great ultimate movement that initiates creation. The symbol also represents the two fundamental principles or activities of the universe: yin and yang. Yin is stillness, tranquility, flexibility, receptivity, femininity, withdrawal, darkness, and cold. Yang is movement, expansion, activity, strength, initiative, masculinity, light, and heat. In a striking contrast to most Western cultures, for Lao-tze and other early Taoists, the feminine and yielding yin was seen as the more useful of the two activities.[69] The interpenetration of the two principles in the t'ai-chi symbol represents "yang embracing yin…Because everything is interrelated, change in one thing will lead to change in others."[70]

Figure 2.1: T'ai-chi symbol

THE CONCEPT OF GOD

For people in a Judeo-Christian culture, the Eastern concepts often raise one obvious question: "Is this universal force the same as God?" The answer to this question depends upon which system of Eastern psychology one refers to. In general, Hinduism contains monistic and polytheistic elements, and as a result, the concept of god can be confusing.

The first difficulty concerns which sacred text one takes as a reference source. Most translations of the classical texts on Hinduism and yoga will often refer to Brahman as "God." In a number of instances, this reference comes from the oldest sacred writings of India such as the *Veda* or the *Upanishads*. Later in the *Bhagava-gita*, Brahman is seen less as God, in the sense of an omnipotent being, and more as the underlying boundless creative force of the universe.[71] Huston Smith has said that in Hinduism, the chief attributes of God depend upon how this ultimate force is portrayed. He says:

> God's relation to the world likewise varies according to the symbolism that is embraced. Conceived in personal terms, God will stand in relation to the world as an artist to his or her handiwork. God will be Creator (Brahma), Preserver (Vishnu), and Destroyer (Shiva), who in the end resolves all finite forms back into the primordial nature from which they sprang. On the other hand, conceived transpersonally, God stands above the struggle, aloof from the finite in every respect.[72]

In Hinduism, there is also the concept of the god within or the god in each person—indeed, in every living element of the universe. As mentioned before, this idea is called the Atman, or the "self-luminous, abiding point of the transpersonal god."[73]

It is interesting to note that Huston Smith describes God as either male or female in the above quote. In Eastern psychology, it is common to find God or gods symbolized as either men or women. For example, in Southeast Asia, the bodhisattva of compassion is called Avalokitesvara and is symbolized as a man; but in Tibet, China, Japan, and other countries, this same bodhisattva is called Kwan-yin and is depicted as a woman (see Photo 2.1).[74]

Photo 2.1: Kwan-yin, the bodhisattva of compassion.

The second difficulty with discussions of God is that the sacred writings of the East have always had a very obvious metaphorical character to them. While the stories may appear to be about gods and people, it is easy to see the use of these literary characters to represent something else. The Hindu trinity, for instance, consists of Brahma, who is the first principle of energy and therefore the god of creation (note: this god is not the same as Brahman); Vishnu, who is the god of preservation; and Shiva (also called Rudra), who is the god of destruction, or the force that returns all things to their fundamental nature.[75] They are gods, however, in the sense that they represent basic foundational powers in the universe. On a more psychological level, the gods also represent similar qualities within the human personality. Photo 2.2 shows Nataraj, the dancing form of Lord Shiva, who represents the rhythm and harmony of life as a cosmic dance, involving both destruction and creation. In human terms, Nataraj represents the potential within every person to destroy illusions and create enlightenment. As was mentioned in chapter 1, the *Bhagavad-Gita* appears to be a story about a dialogue between Arajuna and Krishna before an upcoming battle. In actuality, the text is a metaphor

(handwritten margin notes, left): death = a return to fundamental nature — pureness bliss, peace, oneness

(handwritten margin notes, right): the gods are metaphorical — representing foundational powers in the universe

for the conflicting desires and emotions that accompany the process of spiritual transformation.[76]

Photo 2.2: Nataraj, the dancing form of Lord Shiva.

The third difficulty that comes with any discussion of gods is that as systems of Eastern psychology developed over time and expanded into different cultures, they tended to develop expressions removed from the original intent—expressions that were more compatible with institutionalized forms of religion. In these institutionalized forms, one can find gods worshipped as separate entities that may grant favors and supply good fortune. For instance, today in some sects of Buddhism, the Buddha is prayed to as an omniscient being who will grant favors. This is in spite of the fact that Buddhism is a religion that promotes self-determination and taking personal responsibility for one's own spiritual development. This deification of the Buddha also contradicts that fact that Buddhism has been referred to as a religion that has no concept of God. In fact, Buddhism is unique among world religions in that the Buddha rejected most forms of metaphysical speculation. Instead, he focused on the practical methods that people might use to free themselves and others from discontent and unhappiness. He urged his disciples to not waste time in speculative pursuits but to work toward their own liberation and that of other people.

The Buddha on Metaphysical Speculation A famous story of the Buddha is often quoted to illustrate his rejection of metaphysical speculations, such as whether God exists or not. As the story goes, one of the Buddha's disciples continuously asked for the answers to philosophical and metaphysical questions. The Buddha refused to answer and likened this speculation to a man who has been shot by an arrow. The wounded man insists that before the arrow can be removed he must know who shot it, what type of bow was used, who made the arrow, and all other details of the incident. The Buddha pointed out that the man would die before he exhausted all his questions. Instead, the Buddha said that the questions were irrelevant. What was necessary was to pull out the arrow and solve the basic problem.

For us, then, the basic problem is how to find true happiness and lasting peace of mind. Metaphysical speculation is an unnecessary distraction. Similarly, in Taoism, the question of the origin of things and the existence of a creator are both dismissed as being irrelevant to a search for the Tao.[77] Fundamentally, at the core of Buddhism and Taoism, there is no concept of an omniscient creator God who reigns over the universe.

IS THERE A CONCEPT OF HELL IN EASTERN PSYCHOLOGY?

Related to the previous discussion is the Eastern perspective on hell. It may be surprising to hear that the core teachings of the contemplative traditions in Hinduism, Buddhism, and Taoism do not postulate a concept of hell as is known in the West—a place of everlasting punishments where one's soul may be condemned after death. As Huston Smith has said, "[In the East] the world is ultimately benign. It has no permanent hell and threatens no eternal damnation. It may be loved without fear…all may be loved provided they are not dallied over indefinitely."[78] However, the idea of karma does provide for negative consequences for one's actions, those consequences are not permanent and can be reversed by actions in future lives.

The Hindu perspective sees this life as a place where the dance of life can be enjoyed fully. To be alive in the world is not to suffer punishment for Original Sin. It is not a place to suppress one's desires in hope of a better life in heaven after death. This life is a training ground, where people can actualize their highest capacities for joy and bliss. A person learns about life by experiencing it. Theoretically, after seeing for oneself the limitations of a life based on self-centered hedonism, the person will gladly and naturally let go of hedonistic and self-centered pursuits while turning toward a more spiritual approach to living.[79] That is, there is no need to force people toward a spiritual life. If people are allowed to live life fully, they will inevitably experience the limitations of a nonspiritual orientation to living. As this process happens, people will naturally leave their old orientation behind and can joyfully embrace a spiritual life.

As with the concept of God, however, the secular and popular religions do speak of an underworld or hell. In popular Buddhism, hell is ruled by the god Yama, but it is purgatorial, so that once the ripening of karma is complete, the person may be reborn in a higher realm.[80] The *Tibetan Book of the Dead* is based on the idea of the bardos, which are transitional states between death and the next rebirth. For some, frightful visions can occur in the bardo state as a result of their karma. Popular Taoism also speaks of a heaven, in which the immortals and the fully enlightened sages lived. It also describes *fengdu*, or the underworld, which is ruled by gods who decide the fate of humans after they die.

THE ROOTS OF UNHAPPINESS

In a general sense, Eastern psychologies all tend to agree that the source of human unhappiness can be traced back to a separation from the ultimate reality. The primary source of all human unhappiness and dissatisfaction in the world stems from the fact that as human beings, we do not recognize our fundamental connection to this ultimate wellspring of joy, peace, and bliss. Further, it is assumed that at some relatively unconscious level, everyone recognizes his or her innate connection to this fundamental reality and longs to reconnect with it. Therefore, the fundamental and innate source of motivation, or the most basic need, in everyone's life is a spiritual drive to experience the joy and bliss that occurs when reconnecting with the fundamental reality of the universe. Of course, what everyone wants at the most basic level is liberation from suffering and unhappiness, which is accomplished by reconnecting with the fundamental reality. Unfortunately, most people remain unaware that this basic drive for happiness must involve a spiritual quest.

In Hinduism, the existential malaise in our lives is caused by a failure to recognize the presence of Brahman in our lives and a failure to experience our intimate connection with that reality. Buddhists would say that because we fail to experience the reality of sunyata, we cling to a false sense of reality and suffer. In Taoism, human struggle is due to a failure to align oneself with the universal force of the Tao and allow the Tao to guide our actions in life. Since the Tao is also the way of human life, when life is aligned with Tao, it is how it should be.

As any final state of happiness or peace of mind depends upon a connection with this ultimate reality, most people lead lives that are filled with a sense of unfulfillment or unease. In Hinduism and Buddhism, this sense of unease is called *duhkha* (DEW-*ka*), which is usually translated as "suffering." This sense of suffering includes the normal sources of human pain and misery, but it goes beyond them to an underlying, nagging feeling that a permanent sense of security and peace of mind eludes us.

In yoga psychology, there are five major causes of suffering and unhappiness: ignorance, desire, aversion, egoism, and fear created by the survival instinct. Ignorance (*avidya*) or unconsciousness refers to not knowing our true relationship to the ultimate reality. It is being unaware of our innate spiritual birthright. Even worse, it is not even being curious to know about the relationship. Desire or grasping is a longing for pleasure, and aversion is the recoiling from pain. Egoism (*asmita*) refers to an overidentification with the body and mind. It is associating who we are with our current physical body and our sense of self and identity. Both of these can create unhealthy attachments to anything that will help increase pleasure or decrease pain. Finally, the survival instinct refers to the fear of death. In yoga psychology, this fear comes

from misidentifying with the physical body and ,
rather than identifying with the universal reality (

In Buddhist psychology, the cause of our unhap
in the Four Noble Truths, which were the first publi
Buddha after his final enlightenment. The First Nobl
is suffering. The Buddha meant that we can never esca   .y of
suffering in our lives (see *duhkha* above). Existentialist p   osophers in
the West have made a similar observation. The Second Noble Truth is
that suffering is caused by grasping or attempting to hold on to whatever we believe will bring us security and release from fear. Grasping is
fueled by ignorance, greed (or desire), and anger (or aversion). These
three are defined in essentially the same way as their counterparts in
yoga psychology (see above). The Third Noble Truth is that letting go of
our grasping will bring relief from suffering. The meaning of this Truth
will be described as we move through this chapter. The Fourth Noble
Truth is that the way to let go of our grasping is to practice the Noble
Eightfold Path or the eight steps of liberation. This Noble Truth will be
covered more completely in chapter 4.

THE EVERYDAY WORLD AN ILLUSION

As suggested by the analysis of what causes our unhappiness, the
different Eastern psychologies all agree that most people live their lives
with a normal waking consciousness that is untrained. Even when people
are able to focus their consciousness on a task, the object of that focus
usually creates the wrong goals in life. Further, they are unaware of how
this untrained consciousness is the source of unhappiness. An untrained
consciousness cannot be aware of the innate connection to the ultimate
reality; therefore, we take everyday reality as fundamental and the only
true reality. In contrast, most Eastern perspectives on mental health view
the experience of everyday social reality as an "illusion" and compare it
to "a waking dream" that lacks the depth, insight, and intensity of the
fully experienced spiritual reality. In Hinduism and Buddhism, the term
often used for this illusion is *maya* (MAI-ya).

The use of the word *illusion* does not refer to the idea that objects
in life are somehow not real—that is, that we could walk through solid
rock if we were only enlightened. Rather, the idea of maya refers to how

nstruct and create our psychological perceptions, assumptions, our nse of reality, our worldview, and our sense of personal identity. More specifically, the idea of maya is primarily directed at our psychological perceptions of the self, of our identity, and at our fundamental sense of who we are as individuals. It is assumed that the limited nature of our internal awareness limits our experiential understanding of these self-perceptions. In a manner similar to the Socratic dictum to "know thyself," Eastern psychologies ask us to explore the fundamental nature of our sense of self by deepening our awareness of this fundamental psychological process.

In the Buddhist perspective, when we actually look extremely deeply at the nature of the self, or at how we create a sense of reality, we will eventually discover that it is possible to perceive the world without any illusions, presuppositions or assumptions. This is another way to describe emptiness. Buddhist monk Thanissaro Bhikkhu puts it this way:

> Emptiness is a mode of perception, a way of looking at experience. It adds nothing to and takes nothing away from the raw data of physical and mental events. You look at events in the mind and the senses with no thought of whether there's anything lying beneath them. This mode is called emptiness because it's empty of the presuppositions we usually add to experience to make sense of it: the stories and world-views we fashion to explain who we are and the world we live in. Although these stories have their uses...they get in the way when we try to solve the problem of suffering.[81]

Western psychiatrist and Zen meditation teacher Barry Magid has described emptiness by referring to the ever-changing nature of reality in the following way:

> We can get clearer about the Buddhist position if we recall that "empty" in the jargon of Buddhist metaphysics means lacking any fixed, unchanging, inner, or fundamental essence. So having no "self" actually implies only that whatever we take the self to be, it is constantly changing.[82]

All Eastern psychologies posit that because we are unaware of how our perceptions of self and reality are limited, we are unprepared to adequately solve the problem of human unhappiness. In some ways we are like people who are trying unsuccessfully to put together a jigsaw puzzle and are unaware that they do not have all the pieces to the puzzle. Alan Watts, one of the earliest translators of Eastern thought for Westerners, expresses the eastern point of view by saying:

> Oriental psychology…is concerned, not with the peculiar frustrations of the neurotic individual, but with the general frustration, the common unhappiness (*duhkha* in Sanskrit), which afflicts almost every member of society.
> Buddhist and Hindu psychology agree in ascribing this general unhappiness to *avidya*—a Sanskrit term for a special type of ignorance or unconsciousness, which is the failure to perceive that certain desires and activities are self-contradictory and "viciously circular." The victims of *avidya* are thus described as being in a state of *samsara*—the "round" or "whirl"—a life pattern which, having set itself a self-contradictory goal, revolves or oscillates interminably to the increasing discomfiture of those involved….One of the simplest examples [of this] self-contradiction is the making of one's life goal the acquisition of pleasure and the avoidance of pain.[83]

This is not to say that happiness is impossible in this life. All Eastern psychologies agree that happiness, joy, and even bliss are possible in this life. In fact, as mentioned earlier, Hinduism urges people to enjoy life to the fullest. What is at issue here is the type of happiness that people ultimately seek in their lives. Most of the avenues for happiness pursued by people offer only a temporary and limited sense of well-being. That is, most people pursue relatively superficial and insubstantial forms of happiness. These forms of well-being depend on other internal and external conditions remaining constant in order for happiness to be maintained. That is, if there is an unwanted change in the supportive conditions, then happiness disappears.

Therefore, the basic assumption of all Eastern psychologies is that the normal methods of achieving happiness in life may offer temporary satisfactions and joys but will not lead to ultimate satisfaction or lasting peace of mind. This would even apply to recent work on happiness and subjective well-being found in positive psychology. Eastern psychologies would suggest that efforts to find happiness by promoting and fostering positive emotions are a step in the right direction, but will create a limited perspective on which to build an unshakable peace of mind. Instead, the Eastern psychologies focus on actualizing a specific type of spiritual awakening that leads to optimal states of well-being and optimal personality development.

It may help to note that Western psychology also accepts the general notion that people create their own sense of reality and self-identity. In Western psychology, a number of ideas such as self-verification, self-enhancement, positive illusions, and defense mechanisms all suggest that we are partially responsible for creating the reality of our own self-perceptions. Further, these concepts suggest that those creations may be somewhat distorted by unrecognized needs—or even totally inaccurate. Similarly, studies in cultural anthropology and philosophy also illustrate how we create a sense of reality. Therefore, the idea that people create a sense of reality and a sense of identity that may be inaccurate is found in both Eastern and Western psychologies. Eastern psychology, however, takes this idea much further and explores it in ways that Western intellectual thought has generally not attempted.

THE ROOTS OF TRUE HAPPINESS

The next obvious questions concern what happens when a person experiences a connection with this ultimate spiritual reality—when someone has a mystical experience. When a person has a deep experience of their connection to ultimate reality, they usually report profoundly positive emotions. For most people, these moments are the most meaningful experiences of their lives. As with many emotional experiences in life, the intensity of the experience can range from relatively mild to extraordinarily profound. In his book *Unitive Experiences*, psychologist Gerald May described one such experience in the following way:

> Everything in the immediate environment is experienced with awesome clarity, and the vast panorama of consciousness lies open.

For the duration of the experience—which is usually not long—
mental activity seems to be suspended. Preoccupations, misgiv-
ings, worries, and desires all seem to evaporate, leaving everything
"perfect, just as it is." Usually there are some reactive feelings that
occur toward the end of the experience, feelings such as awe, wonder,
expansiveness, freedom, warmth, love, and a sense of total truth or
"rightness." After the experience is over, there is an almost invariable
recollection of having been *at one*.[84]

W. T. Stace suggested that there were two basic forms that mystical
experiences could take. The first form is extrovertive mysticism. In this
form, the person feels as if she or he has become one with the universe,
feels a deep unity among all things, has merged with something greater,
or experiences a unity consciousness. The person may feel a sense of
the sacred in all life as well as profound joy, but an altered sense of self-
identity may be maintained during the experience. People perceive that
they are not separate from their environment; their consciousness seems
to merge with their surroundings as the usual ego boundaries between
self and other are briefly dissolved. That is, people describe a felt sense of
connection to a larger reality that is less defined by egocentric perceptions,
personal needs, and the usual psychological divisions between our sense
of self and others.

The second form is introvertive mysticism. In this type, the person feels as if he or she has been absorbed into a consciousness that is
beyond space and time. The person has an experience that seems impossible to put into words. It may be beyond content and form—it may be,
in fact, more like a void, because it is so removed from any conceptual
category that could possibly be placed upon it. Stace also assumed that
the extrovertive and introvertive forms of mysticism were simply different expressions of a common core mystical experience. This core could
be found in all mystical experiences, whether in Eastern or Western
religions.

In Taoism it is said that a person must identify with the Tao by
inward realization of its unity, simplicity, and emptiness. All desires
must subside and the senses must withdraw to a completely interior
point of focus. The *Tao Te Ching* says "empty yourself of everything"
and "returning to the source is serenity." The result is a "condition of

alert waiting known as 'sitting with a blank mind'." When the spiritual realization arrives, with it comes a sense of truth, joy, and completion. It is said that "everything at last falls into place…creating a joy unlike any hitherto known."[85]

As mentioned above, people report these experiences as the most satisfying emotional experiences of their lives. Most report dramatic changes in how they create meaning in life as a consequence of intense spiritual experiences. Much of the spiritual significance that people experience seems to be directly related to the subsequent sense of merging between the individual self and a larger spiritual reality.

ENLIGHTENMENT AND NIRVANA

In the Eastern psychologies, there are a number of terms for the mystical experience. Probably the two most familiar to Westerners are *enlightenment* and *nirvana*. Someone who has experienced a connection to the ultimate reality has had an *enlightenment* experience.[86] In Hinduism and Buddhism, the word enlightenment comes from the Sanskrit term *bodhi*, which means "awakened."[87] To experience enlightenment is to "wake up" from maya, or the illusion of the world as we normally know it. After enlightenment, the person is now aware of, or awake to, the ultimate reality that lies behind the illusions of the normal world. A person can have numerous enlightenment experiences, each of which may be deeper with more profound insights. In Buddhism, it is assumed that the person who had the deepest and most profound enlightenment experience possible was the Buddha. In fact, the term "Buddha" is an honorific one, meaning the "enlightened" or "awakened" one. In the West, it is common to hear certain spiritual teachers referred to as an "enlightened" person. Unfortunately, this descriptor is quite vague, because it says nothing about the depth of the experiences the person has had or the subsequent wisdom the person possesses.

The term *nirvana* has a somewhat more technical meaning. Recall that Eastern psychologies assume that we are blinded to the ultimate reality, because our desires keep us attached to illusions about reality and self. Eastern psychologies assume it is possible to experience the complete extinction of desire, attachment, or grasping as the basis for one's life. In Sanskrit, this experience is called *nirvana*, or "the extinction of thirst." That is, to realize nirvana is to be released from all needs and desires based on clinging—especially greed, anger, and delusion, which are the building blocks of attachment.[88] The realization of nirvana is accompanied by profound positive emotions. Buddhist monk and scholar Walpola Rahula says, "He who has realized the Truth, Nirvana, is the happiest being in the world....He is joyful...free from anxiety, serene and peaceful...full of universal love, compassion, kindness, sympathy, understanding and tolerance."[89] Again, Alan Watts can be instructive:

> For according to Hindu and Buddhist teachings the enlightened man attains a state of mind that is one with the reality of life....This state is non-dualistic because it is a union with something to which nothing can be opposed, and in this sense it is complete and absolute acceptance of life.[90]

Although there are some doctrinal differences between the terms *enlightenment* and *nirvana* among various schools of Hinduism and Buddhism, practically speaking, many people consider the terms to be relatively synonymous with each other.[91] Nevertheless, it may be interesting to note how subtle differences present themselves. In Hinduism, the experience of enlightenment is said to allow a union with the Absolute, Brahman, or God. In Buddhism, there is no self or soul to create a union. Therefore, nirvana refers to a realization that there is no self or soul and, therefore, the experience is seen as the complete cessation of attachments and clinging.

THE OPTIMAL PERSONALITY IN EASTERN PSYCHOLOGY

Certainly one of the most striking features found in descriptions of deep spiritual experiences is the profound positive emotions used to describe the experiences. For instance, Zen teacher Claire Myer Owens says, "The bliss and awe of enlightenment are indescribable...The enlightened person feels as if realization of the Self answers all questions, dispels all doubts, abolishing fear and anger, hate and jealousy. It ends alienation."[92]

Descriptions such as this are common in Eastern psychological literature. However, it is not the cultivation of positive emotions per se that is the goal of Eastern disciplines. More than any specific emotional state, the goal involves a transformation of self-identity and personality. In Eastern psychologies, it is assumed that a serious, dedicated spiritual practice will result in a fairly consistent set of personality and behavioral changes.

In Buddhism, these changes are classified under the two major headings of wisdom and compassion. Wisdom is discovered through insights into the ultimate nature of reality. Compassion encompasses the various changes in emotionality, such as increased altruism, empathy, and a sense of universal love. The Taoist sage Chuang-tzu wrote about the ideal of *chih-jen,* or the perfected human being. The Taoists believe this person has fully realized his or her unity with the Tao, has transcended all psychological limitations, and has attained perfect freedom. His or her life is perfectly attuned to and balanced with the natural forces of nature. This person reacts to any situation effortlessly.[93] Lynne Hagen says that such a person "cooperates with the course of the natural world...[just like the] patterns found in water and wood...[and is] mindful of the natural rhythms of nature, knows and trusts one's inner self, and lives fully in the present."[94]

In Taoism, the purpose of human life—and the way to true happiness—lies in aligning our lives to the forces in nature, which are an expression of the *Tao.* A number of the personality traits that are associated with the enlightened sage can be found in the term *wu wei* (woo-WAY), which is often translated as "nonaction." This is not passivity, but rather allowing the Tao to guide one's life without resistance. Actions done in the spirit of wu wei combine two contradictory qualities: effective action and supreme relaxation. Huston Smith describes it by saying:

> *Wu wei* is the supreme action, the precious suppleness, simplicity, and freedom that flows from us, or rather through us, when our private egos and conscious efforts yield to a power that is not their own...Taoism's approach is...to get the foundation of the self in tune with *Tao* and let behavior flow spontaneously. Action follows being; new action follows new being, wiser being, stronger being.

The *Tao Te Ching* puts this point without wasting a word, "The way to do," it says, "is to be."[95]

Another main concept in Taoism is that of *te*. Te is often translated as virtue or power (note: *Tao "Te" Ching* or *The Way and Its "Power"*). However, the term does not refer to power as dominance over others. Rather, te refers to strength that comes by expressing the virtues and internal psychological qualities necessary to fully experience the Tao in one's life. Therefore, te suggests the correct way to live life in accordance with the Tao.

A similar ideal in Taoism is that of *p'u*, or natural simplicity. This ideal is often referred to as "the uncarved block," or the original nature of things before they are tampered with by ideas, concepts, or other man-made creations. The ideal state for the Taoist is to recapture this original naturalness and simplicity to relate harmoniously with others, nature, and the Tao.

Taoist philosophy frequently takes images from nature. The most frequently used metaphor is that of water. The water in a stream or river finds its own way without undue effort, regardless of the obstacles. It works without working; without effort it accomplishes what it needs to do in congruity with natural law. The ideal is a profound naturalness, simplicity, and attunement with nature that results in a sense of absolute tranquility.[96]

IS THE GOAL TO GET RID OF THE EGO?

Writers on Eastern psychology often use the terms *ego* and *self* interchangeably. Unfortunately, this is a misleading use of these terms. When many people describe the goal of Eastern psychologies, they state it is to get rid of the ego or the self. This is not entirely accurate. Buddhist monk and scholar Walpola Rahula states, "Nirvana is definitely no annihilation of self, because there is no self to annihilate. If at all, it is the annihilation of the illusion, of the false idea of self."[97] Taking a somewhat different approach with his presentation of Buddhist psychology, psychiatrist Mark Epstein says that it is only one component of the Freudian ego that is deemed illusory. He states:

It is not ego, in the Freudian sense that is the actual target of the Buddhist insight, it is, rather, the self-concept, the representational component of the ego, the actual internal experience of one's self that is targeted. The point is that the entire ego is not transcended; the self-representation is revealed as lacking concrete existence. It is not the case of something real being eliminated, but of the essential groundlessness being realized for what it has always been.[98]

Epstein is saying that when the eastern perspective speaks of the dissolution of the self-other boundary, it is not saying that people return to a childlike state of merger with the environment, prior to the formation of a self-concept. They are not referring to regression or a return to the oceanic feeling of the womb that Sigmund Freud believed it represented. They are also not saying that the mechanisms of our psychological life, which coordinates internal and external perceptions, are abandoned—that would be psychosis and chaos. Rather, they are saying that once the self-concept is formed, we all believe that our sense of "I" has a real and permanent existence, much like the chair we sit on or the desk we write on. It is this belief in the unchanging and fundamental ontological reality of the self-identity that is the illusion.

The Eastern perspective postulates that when we fully experience the representational self-concept for what it actually is—a dynamic, fluid, and adapting collection of sense impressions, memories, and awareness—and when we fully experience that reality now, then that insight can foster greater psychological well-being. However, seeing through the illusion of self-identity often requires considerable effort. Frequently, the iconography depicts images from battle to represent the effort needed. Photo 2.3 shows a statue of Manjusri, a bodhisattva associated with transcendental wisdom. In his right hand he holds a sword used to powerfully cut through ignorance, delusion, and the false sense of self.

Photo 2.3: Manjusri, the bodhisattva of transcendental wisdom.

Benefits from an Insight into Selflessness How would this perception of the world and the self be beneficial? First, a profound insight into the temporality of the self could lead to a reorientation, such that openness to experience and living life in the moment were more important than defensiveness, rigidity, and self-absorption. Often this is expressed as exhilaration and joy in the simple activities of life. Second, the unshakable knowledge that self and other were part of a larger spiritual whole could lead to compassion, empathy, tolerance, and other altruistic emotions and behaviors. After all, if your own experience has told you in rather dramatic terms that you and another person are "one," it is much more difficult to do them harm or to pursue relatively selfish goals in life. Finally, the fear of death could be radically diminished, along with the basic guilt and anxiety that many existentialists consider foundational and irrevocable.

On the other hand, it seems that for many people, it would be terrifying to suddenly perceive that "you" were not real. In fact, the experience without a necessary context in which to understand it can be very confusing.[99] I remember meeting someone who had a very deep and profound spontaneous mystical experience a number of years earlier. The usual boundaries between self and not-self had vanished, but he was extremely confused by the experience. Neither his minister nor various psychotherapists were able to explain the experience, so he began an intense search for an answer. Months later, his search took him to a Japanese Zen master, who understood the experience and could give him a context in which to comprehend what had happened to him. Only at that point did the memory of the experience become a source of new meaning and new direction for his life.

TOTAL TRANSFORMATION OF THE PERSONALITY

Probably the most incredulous assumption of Eastern psychology to psychologists trained in the West has been the idea that negative emotions and behaviors can be *totally* eliminated. However, Eastern psychology is quite serious about this claim. That is, Eastern psychology posits that it is possible to completely transform one's personality, behavior, and emotional responses to life such that one experiences and acts from a sense of universal compassion and love. Of course, after a single enlightenment experience, the personality is altered only slightly. I recall speaking about this to a Japanese Zen master. He said that after each enlightenment experience, "a small portion of my brain is permanently changed," never to return to how it was before.

Eastern psychologies are based on the idea that after repeated enlightenment experiences and disciplined spiritual training, a total and permanent transformation of the personality is possible. In Theravada Buddhism, someone who has achieved this psychological transformation is referred to as an *arhat* (ARE-hot).[100] Daniel Goleman states:

> The *arhat* embodies the essence of mental health in [Buddhist psychology]. His personality traits are permanently altered; all his motives, perceptions, and actions that he formerly engaged in under the influence of unhealthy factors will have vanished.... While the *arhat* may seem virtuous beyond belief from the perspective of Western psychology, he embodies characteristics common to the ideal type in most every Asian psychology. The *arhat* is the

enlightened being, a prototype notable in the main for its absence in Western personality theory.[101]

The only partial equivalent to the idea of the arhat in the West is the Catholic idea of a saint.[102] In traditional Western psychological theory, however, the total transformation of personality assumed possible in the East is almost never even considered.

In Hinduism and Buddhism, it is assumed that the practice of meditation results in a number of predictable personality changes. The core qualities can be found listed as the *Brahma-Viharas*. The *Brahma-Viharas* are the four "sublime states," "heavenly abodes," or universal virtues.[103] These are qualities by which an enlightened being or bodhisattva can be recognized. Students of meditation deliberately put into practice these virtues as a way to actualize them in their lives. The *Brahma-Viharas* are as follows:

(1) equanimity or peacefulness in vicissitudes of life
(2) loving-kindness and goodwill toward all beings
(3) compassion or mercy
(4) sympathetic or altruistic joy—especially for the happiness and success of others

The Seven Factors of Enlightenment in Buddhism present a similar list:
(1) mindfulness   (5) concentration
(2) energy   (6) tranquility
(3) investigation   (7) equanimity [104]
(4) rapture

In Taoism, the enlightened Sage exhibits eight characteristics:
(1) humbleness   (5) adaptability
(2) simplicity   (6) spontaneity
(3) genuineness   (7) persistence
(4) flexibility   (8) acceptance [105]

Michael Stark and Michael Washburn speculated on what personality traits might be found in someone who had achieved a high level of spiritual realization in either an Eastern or a Western contemplative spiritual discipline.[106] The eight traits they listed were the following:

(1) an adventuresome sense of life
(2) a sense of tranquility
(3) a frequent experience of bliss
(4) nonattachment, or the ability to let go of barriers and limitations
(5) the ability to bring presence and absorption to all everyday experiences
(6) openness to experience
(7) high resilience
(8) a sense of spontaneity

These lists seem to combine a sense of spiritual peace, equanimity, openness to the experiences of life, compassion, naturalness, high adaptability, and spontaneity.

THE PARADOX OF USING EFFORT TO "LET GO"

To review, the presentation so far has discussed the theory of well-being and mental health as expressed in Eastern psychology, which begins with an explanation of why it is so difficult to find lasting and deeply fulfilling happiness—a lack of connection to the ultimate reality. It goes on to present a solution to the problem—we need to connect with the ultimate reality by altering perceptions of self and transcending unhealthy desires. It then offers effective intervention strategies that will implement the solution—meditation and other spiritual practices. So far, it all seems fairly straightforward.

However, one of the most intriguing aspects of Eastern theories of well-being is that they warn us that most of our usual efforts to find happiness are, in fact, the *primary cause* of our discomfort! Eastern psychology postulates that our normal attempts to completely control life in order to experience happiness and avoid pain will turn out to be the *basic cause* of our suffering and discomfort. All Eastern psychologies agree that our usual efforts to obtain lasting happiness may actually increase our sense of discomfort and anxiety. The more we try to "control" life, "manage" stress, "balance" our responsibilities, or "actualize" our potentials, the more we fight against the inevitability of constant change. That is, all these efforts ignore that fact that without question, everyone's life must include unwelcome and undesirable events. In fact, life will ultimately result in the final insult to all our efforts at control—our own death.

In a traditional Western approach, it is assumed that optimal well-being is associated with a positive sense of self-esteem and can be found by strengthening and maintaining a person's coping skills, cultivating meaningful goals, fostering healthy positive emotions, maintaining mutually supportive interpersonal relationships, and increasing a sense of meaning and purpose in life. Although Eastern psychology does not deny that this strategy can be very helpful, it nonetheless does assert that this strategy will not lead to *true* happiness or *final* peace of mind. The problem is that these strategies are based on illusions about the nature of the self and on efforts at control that are bound to fail eventually. The goal of Eastern psychology is how to achieve a *final* sense of liberation from human suffering, a sense that remains constant in the face of difficulty, disappointment, and even death.

From an Eastern perspective, the problem with the traditional approach of Western psychology lies in the fact that it is ultimately based on fear. It is driven by the fear that without constant vigilance, some negative emotion or experience will intrude upon an otherwise happy and stress-free life. However, as life is ultimately not under anyone's personal control, the approach is self-defeating. At its core, the Western strategy involves an unrelenting conflict between the maintenance of positive experiences and the constant threat of negative emotions. All efforts are focused on ensuring that we live "happily ever after," that emotional pain does not intrude into our lives and the lives of those we love. In his book, *The Meaning of Happiness,* Alan Watts portrays the conflict at the heart of this issue:

> Thus we have two psychological states called "acceptance of life" and "escape from life," but when they are opposed to one another in this way it is clear that "life" can have only a limited meaning. It means particular things in life, [however] everything is life, even escapism, and if the whole of life is to be accepted the desire to escape must not be made into a new devil. Therefore partial acceptance is

what Oriental philosophers would describe as dualistic as distinct from a non-dualistic state of mind....

But [a] total acceptance and love of life eludes us because in striving to attain it we are constantly at war with that which appears to go against it. The reason is that in trying to be united with life we are striving to achieve something that already exists; the result is that our very efforts to achieve it are hindrances in that they encourage the [false] feeling that we are divorced from life and have to make ourselves one with it.[107]

Watts states the basic paradox at the heart of any mental health intervention, which is that any attempt to directly and purposefully eliminate all negative experiences from life is ultimately self-defeating for two reasons. First, the goal is impossible to accomplish—no one can completely control life. Second, the effort is based on a duality of positive versus negative experiences that forces us to run away from some elements of life. The culmination of meditation practice in nirvana and enlightenment requires a transcendence of all dualities. Any purposeful effort to eliminate negative emotions only strengthens the basic duality of positive and negative. It's like one of those frustrating Chinese finger puzzles that only grip tighter the more you try to pull them off your finger. What makes this so perplexing is that some people will assert that the goal of the Eastern psychology is ultimate "happiness" or "bliss."

A way out of this paradox is to transcend the apparent opposites of the duality. Like the yin/yang symbol of Taoism, each side of the duality is necessary for the other, and they also interpenetrate each other. The whole or the totality must include both sides. Actually, most people acknowledge that both the positive and negative aspects of life should be accepted in some way. Most people know that a rich and full life, a life of significance and meaning, must somehow embrace both the joys and the struggles of life. Most people, however, are not quite sure just how to accomplish this feat. Lama Govinda has said:

[S]piritual development does not so much consist in the *solution* of our problems, as in growing *beyond* them....The Buddha, therefore...insisted that everybody should be his own lamp, should find his own way, realize the Dharma [Truth] within himself by going beyond the problems which ordinary intellect has ever failed to solve, and which can be overcome alone by "bodhicitta" [intrinsic wisdom], the highest type of consciousness.[108]

We solve the paradox of working hard to "let go" by seeing the larger context and the complete interdependence of each side. We must nurture acceptance rather than avoidance and awareness rather than denial. Alan Watts once again provides a clear explanation of the puzzling paradox:

> [However, in the enlightened state of mind] man is supremely happy because even though he may be involved in a conflict with pain and evil, even though he may feel the very human emotions of fear, anger, and love, he lives his life with a wholeheartedness and abandon born of the understanding that all things are fundamentally acceptable. For him there is meaning and divinity in every aspect of the universe and in both the greatness and the littleness, the love and the fear, the joy and the sorrow, and the content and discontent of the human soul.[109]

THE SACRED AND THE SECULAR ARE IDENTICAL

A final point also needs to be mentioned about well-being. Throughout this discussion, the cultivation of profound religiously oriented experiences has been discussed repeatedly. This is because these experiences are a major element of Eastern psychology. Techniques such as meditation and yoga are all focused on transforming how people experience the reality of the self, emotional reactions to life events, and consensual ideas about the nature of reality. However, note that this idea can lead to a subtle denigration of the normal world of experiences and an elevation of the spiritual world as "better than" ordinary reality. The late Chogyam Trungpa, a Tibetan Rinpoche, or reincarnated meditation master, referred to this problem as "spiritual materialism." He warned that the pursuit of profound religious experiences can turn into a materialistic quest to simply acquire an exotic collection of emotional experiences.[110] Interestingly, most Eastern perspectives state that the highest levels of spiritual attainment transcend even the duality of sacred versus secular. At the highest levels of spirituality, the adept sees the spiritual world and the ordinary world as not only interdependent, but identical.

For example, in the Zen Buddhist tradition, the Ten Ox Herding Pictures visually depict the path of enlightenment in metaphorical terms. In the pictures, the seeker struggles with his spiritual practice but eventually experiences selflessness and emptiness. The last picture in the series is titled, "the monk re-enters the marketplace."[111] That is, after years of training, the spiritually and psychologically transformed monk returns to participate in the ordinary world, but now with a new spiritual perspective. A famous story from the ninth century illustrates this last stage. The story involves a disciple asking Ch'an master P'ang Chu-Shih what he has learned from meditation. The master replies, "I chop wood, I carry water. How wondrous!"[112] In other words, the simple everyday tasks of chopping wood for the fire and carrying water had become opportunities for joy, awe, and spiritual meaning—life itself as sacrament. The contemporary American Zen teacher Charlotte Joko Beck says she teaches "everyday Zen" or "ordinary Zen."[113] These phrases mean that this life, this everyday body, and this everyday mind are the expression of enlightenment. It's not that the secular is contained inside or embraced by the sacred, but rather the secular and the sacred are the same thing. Further, the goal is not always to retreat to a monastery for the rest of one's life—although some practitioners do just that. Rather, the goal is to be a part of the world with renewed joy and a desire to help other people. Huston Smith expressed this point of view when he said, "The goal, it cannot be stressed too often, is not religious experiences: it is the religious life."[114]

CLOSING THOUGHTS

In summary, in Eastern religions, a sense of well-being is fostered by accepting all aspects of life with equanimity and by finding a spiritual sense of meaning and purpose through insights into the nature of human consciousness.[115] This is achieved through the practices of meditation, which allow for experiencing the world and the self in fundamentally different ways and diminishing the need for traditional goal attainment as a source of happiness, because ultimate happiness is present in each moment. Primarily, this transformation involves a radical change in how the nature of self and identity is perceived as well as by creating a new relationship with one's natural desires and emotional responses. When the concept of a stable and permanent self is seen to be an illusion, this leads to experiencing a oneness with all of reality. With proper training, the experience results in an increase of compassion for others, a release from fear and anxiety, along with a profound spiritual joy. Eastern psychologies agree that this experience is an innate potential that human beings possess, but rarely explore.

Much of what has been presented so far may make for interesting theory, but is there any validity to it? For instance, do people who practice Eastern disciplines show evidence of higher well-being and better mental health? The research to be reviewed later certainly suggests that Eastern techniques and disciplines such as meditation can be associated with increased well-being. In addition, the lives of a small number of great spiritual teachers also suggests that it is possible to conduct a life with selfless compassion, empathy, tolerance, personal dignity, and great composure, even in the face of injustice or death. The examples of the current Dalai Lama and Mother Teresa come immediately to mind. On the other hand, a few gurus, Zen masters, and other spiritual teachers in the West have been involved in unethical behavior, such as sexual relations with students. This suggests that having had enlightenment experiences does not guarantee saint-like behavior, and that the total transformation of personality can be a very lengthy process.

It is also true that the Eastern vision of optimal mental health is not for everyone. First, it can take extraordinary discipline and dedication. Second, it can also present many challenges to the more traditional goals of loving family, good friends, and meaningful work. In the past, full dedication to the Eastern vision often meant a temporary exodus from society to monasteries or temples. Certainly, this is not a solution to a midlife crisis that would appeal to most people.

Finally, the Eastern perspective on optimal mental health may have little to say about psychopathology. In many cases, Western psychotherapy is by far the most appropriate vehicle for dealing with serious psychological problems such as depression, anxiety, or trauma. However, it is also true that techniques of Eastern psychology can be utilized for more relaxation, better health, greater life satisfaction, and as an adjunct to psychotherapy without adopting the metaphysical assumptions or the strict monastic discipline of a committed Eastern approach to happiness. Even those who are fully committed to an Eastern approach to well-being recognize that there are many ways to use the techniques without adopting the life a contemplative monk.[116] However, for those interested in pursuing the Eastern version of optimal mental health in whatever capacity is appropriate, it appears that this perspective can offer a unique and quite satisfying approach.

Before leaving this introduction to the Eastern approaches to well-being and mental health, it may be helpful to get a feel for what this perspective feels like from the inside. As mentioned earlier, the practice of meditation has been fundamental to many Eastern practices for thousands of years. So, in closing this chapter, I would like to quote from Paul Fleischman's wonderful essay, describing what motivates him, as a Western-trained psychiatrist, to meditate:

> Most of our lives are spent in externally oriented functions that distract from self-observation. This restless, obsessive drive persists independently of survival needs such as warmth, and even pleasure...It is striking how many ordinary activities, from smoking a pipe to watching sunsets, veer towards, but ultimately avoid, sustained attention to the reality of our own life. So it is not an intellectual intrigue with Platonic dictum ["know thyself"] that leads me to meditate, but an experience of myself and my fellow humans as stimulus-bound, fundamentally out of control, alive only in reaction.
>
> I want to know, to simply observe, this living person as he is, not just as he appears to be while careening from event to event...My quest for knowing is not merely objective and scientific. This mind-and-body is the vessel of my life. I want to drink its nectar, and if necessary, its sludge, but I want to know it with the same organic emersion that sets a snow goose flying ten thousand miles every winter and spring. It seems to me that the forces of creation, the laws of nature, out of which this mind-and-body arose, must be operative in me now, continuously, and whenever I make an effort to observe them. The activity of creation must be the original and continuing cause of my life.[117]

CHAPTER 3

Personality Theories in Eastern Psychology

Too much pleasure? Yang has too much influence. Too much suffering? Yin has too much influence. When one of these outweighs the other, it is as if the seasons came at the wrong times. The balance of cold and heat is destroyed; the body of man suffers.

CHUANG TZU[118]

When Western psychologists began to study Eastern psychology, they found personality theories that were more complex and more diverse than had previously been recognized in the West. Hidden in the somewhat esoteric writings of Eastern psychology were logically consistent theories that explained how psychological processes are related to thought, emotion, and behavior.

Personality theories in both Western and Eastern psychology try to explain human behavior, thought, and emotion. Practically, most personality theories tend to take a specific focus that allows them to begin explaining behavior. However, usually the specific focus ends up limiting the scope of the theory. For example, Freud began by trying to explain certain types of psychopathology by referring to unconscious processes. His theory goes into great detail when it addresses these areas, but it lacks explanatory power when it tries to explain healthy, positive, adaptive, and self-actualizing behavior. Early behaviorism could explain how pleasure and pain shaped our behavior, but it lacked precision when it came to the impact of thought on behavior. Eastern psychologies focus on what they consider to be optimal well-being. Further, they focus primarily on how thinking and cognitive processes create a sense of reality and our sense of self.

FOUNDATIONS OF PERSONALITY

REINCARNATION

Hinduism and Buddhism both assume that some type of reincarnation is a fundamental reality that partially determines the characteristics of the human personality. The theory of reincarnation says that we have all lived many previous lives. Our behavior in those other lives has created consequences that affect our current life. A portion of who we are today comes to us from how we conducted ourselves in our past lives.

In Hinduism, rebirth can occur in a variety of forms. Although it is possible for the atman or spiritual essence of a person to be reborn in human form, it may also reincarnate into animal forms as well. In fact, rebirth in human form is rare. Since a human reincarnation is the only one in which spiritual progress can occur, being born in human form is seen as a valuable opportunity for spiritual growth.

Since Buddhism does not believe in a permanent essence of the personality or permanent self, it is not the atman that is reincarnated. Rather, it is a "karmically controlled continuity of consciousness" that is transmitted.[119] This different perspective is necessary because Buddhism views the self as a series of dynamic processes, rather than an unchanging spiritual essence. The Buddha used the analogy of a flame being passed from one candle to another to describe the process of rebirth.[120]

Nevertheless, the point is that neither Hinduism nor Buddhism assumes we are born into this world as a blank slate or without any prior inclinations toward personality dispositions. In contrast to Hinduism and Buddhism, Taoism does not typically discuss reincarnation.

THE LAW OF KARMA

The law of karma states that "for every effect there is a cause and for every action there is a reaction."[121] All of our actions create consequences for future behavior. Over time, these consequences accumulate and become a strong force that can determine our behavior. However, Eastern psychology also proposes a way to diminish or eliminate the effects of karma.

Hinduism and Buddhism believe that an action inevitably creates karma only if the person is psychologically attached to the results or the fruits of the action. That is, if a person is psychologically committed to obtaining a specific outcome from the action, then it will create karma. On the other hand, if the person can act in a selfless manner without demanding a specific outcome, then karma is not created. Since karma creates psychological bondage and leads to suffering, the elimination of karma leads to greater well-being. Therefore, self-transcendence and true well-being are nurtured by compassionate selfless actions that burn up accumulated karma. Note that in Western psychology, most perspectives assume that goal-directed behavior designed to meet our needs and desires is essential to greater well-being. In contrast, Eastern psychology assumes this type of normal, goal-directed behavior leads to further karma and creates the endless cycle of rebirth known as the *wheel of karma*.

Types of Karma Over thousands of years, the concept of reincarnation in Hinduism has evolved into a description of three major ways that karma may influence our lives. The first is *prarabda* karma, which is karma created in this life as a result of actions in a former life.[122] Essentially, this is karma that we create now as we try to work out issues from our former lives. The second is *sanchita* karma, which is the karmic deposits we accumulated in past lives that are yet to be worked out in a future life, although they may impact our current life. Interestingly, some have suggested that this idea may have influenced Swiss psychiatrist Carl G. Jung's concept of the collective unconscious. The third type is *agami* karma, which is karma that is created in this life as a result of current actions.

The different types of karma are also central to another element of personality theory. All personality theories attempt to answer why we are compelled to act without thinking in various circumstances. The law of karma states that each thought, emotion or action we experience creates a "seed" in our unconscious or our karmic tally. For instance, if we experience anger, then a seed of anger is created in the unconscious; if we feel envy, then a seed of envy is created. These seeds wait until conditions are right, and then they "sprout" into a new emotion or desire. In other words, each experience helps create the conditions for a reemergence of that same experience. Each time we feel anger, we create the potential for future anger; each experience of envy creates the potential for envy in the future, and so forth.

MOTIVATION AND INNATE DRIVES

ENHANCE PLEASURE AND AVOID PAIN

One major similarity between Eastern and Western psychologies is that each assumes a major motivating factor in life is the drive to find pleasure and avoid pain. Each also assumes that if these motivating factors are not regulated properly, then life becomes a self-destructive search for self-indulgent pleasure. Western psychology, however, tends to look for ways that the innate tendency toward hedonistic self-interest can be channeled into a socially sensitive self-interest that is tied to a concern for others. In the West, it is assumed that if this can be managed and regulated properly, then the appreciation of certain bodily pleasures such as sexuality or culinary delights are enhanced and savored, and the higher pleasures or gratifications such as creativity and aesthetics are cultivated.

As has been mentioned, in Eastern psychology pleasures are to be enjoyed, savored, and cultivated as well. Hinduism, especially, encourages people to enjoy life and savor its pleasures. After all, it was Hinduism that gave the world the famous fifth-century manual of sexual techniques, the *Kama Sutra*.[123] For Eastern psychologies, the problem isn't necessarily pleasure. Instead, the issue is clinging or attaching to pleasure so that it takes on the characteristics of an obsession. The goal in the East is to experience and savor each moment of life and cultivate the ability to let it go without regrets, remorse, or cravings for similar pleasures in the future.

SELF-TRANSCENDENCE

The Eastern psychologies assume a second major source of human motivation. This is an innate drive toward self-transcendence. This drive is expressed as a longing for union with the ultimate reality of the universe; with Brahman, the Void, or the Tao. It is assumed that at some level of awareness, we all know we are separated from the experience of spiritual union. Therefore, we are driven to find the ultimate spiritual peace that we know is part of our birthright. We are driven to find *moksha* (MOKE-sha), or liberation. The tensions between our drives for personal pleasure and the drive for spiritual union define the many ways in which our karma is created in life. When we indulge ourselves in personal pleasures, we bind ourselves to the cycle of rebirths. When we seek the higher spiritual pleasures of union with the ultimate ground, we burn up karma and move ourselves toward ultimate liberation from the cycle of rebirths, or from *samsara* (sahm-SA-ra).

SELF-IDENTITY AND EGO

So far we have seen that Eastern psychology assumes that we have the innate drives to seek pleasure and avoid pain, the seeds of our past karma that direct us in certain psychological and behavioral directions, and the drive for self-transcendence. As we grow and mature from children to adults, one of the hallmarks of the human developmental process is the creation of a sense of self-identity. Note that although this is normally referred to as the development of ego, this is an imprecise term for a multifaceted psychological process. The ego is generally seen as a collection of psychological processes that coordinates our impulses, wishes, and desires with both the demands of the external world and with our internal standards for proper behavior. The self refers to our internal sense of identity as a separate person, as a separate "I" (remember that when the Self is spelled with a capital "S," it refers to the Transcendent Self).

From the standpoint of Eastern psychology, the important element of the functioning ego is the sense of self-identity, or the conviction that we are a permanent "I," which leads a completely separate existence from the rest of the universe. The sense of self, or the sense of I-am-ness, is seen as a psychological process that is useful for adaptation to the world and a natural creation of consciousness—much like our sense of hearing or sight. Nevertheless, the sense of permanent self is viewed as an illusion. It is not that our sense of our own unique self does not exist, or that it has no psychological reality for us. Rather, it is our belief that this self is permanent, unchanging, and the ultimate ground of all our experience that is an illusory fiction. What we call the self is a product of how we combine sense impressions, memories, bodily sensations, and consciousness. In the words of the Buddha:

> Just as when the parts are set together
> There arises the word "chariot",
> So does the notion of a being arise
> When the sensory impressions are present.[124]

A more contemporary example has been given of a film. Although the film is actually a series of still pictures, the speed at which it is projected produces the illusion of movement and obscures the underlying reality of the medium. To extend the metaphor somewhat, people will often watch films and get so caught up in the story that they identify with characters and experience strong emotions to what is essentially a series of still pictures projected rapidly on a screen. In Eastern psychology, there is no "self" that exists inside us—whether real self, ideal self, or true self. There is no self that exists independent of our dynamic, moment-by-moment experiences in consciousness.

Along these same lines, a famous metaphor in Taoism is of the butterfly and the dream. The Taoist sage Chuang Tzu wrote:

> Once I, Chuan Tzu, dreamed I was a butterfly and was happy as a butterfly. Suddenly I awoke and there I was, visibly myself. I do not know whether it was myself dreaming that he was a butterfly or the butterfly dreaming he was me.[125]

The obvious point of the story is that the nature of reality is subjective. Interestingly, this same story of the butterfly dream has been used in Western philosophy to illustrate a similar philosophical position on our perception of reality.

CREATING THE SENSE OF PERSONAL IDENTITY

In general, all Eastern systems agree that our sense of self-identity is created from four very broad areas of awareness, although many finer distinctions are made as well. First, our sense of self comes from awareness of our physical selves or from our bodies and senses. Second, our sense of identity is partially a result of our conscious perceptions, internal cognitions, and emotions. Third, we also have unconscious and subconscious aspects to our lives, where memories and old experiences may be held. So far, Western psychology also agrees that these three are components of our sense of self. Lastly, in Eastern psychology our self is also created from, or is an intimate aspect of, the deeper level of ultimate reality that has been discussed above. In Hinduism, our perception of self-identity, or our internal sense of being a unique personality who "lives inside" our bodies, is termed *asmita,* or I-am-ness (note: the term for the functioning ego is *ahankara*).

PERSONALITY THEORY

The concept of personality types is quite similar in both Eastern and Western psychology. In both systems, a personality type describes consistencies of behavior over time as well as relative uniformity in how a person relates to her or his inner world of experiences.

In Hinduism, there are four fundamental personality types. The first type is the *reflective* personality. People in whom this type predominates tend to be intellectual, thoughtful, and analytic. The second type is the *emotional* personality. This type is associated with using feelings, emotions, and affectivity as guides to operating in the world. The third basic personality type is the *active* type. This type describes people who are focused on practical applications and making an objective impact in the world. Finally, there is the *experimental* type. This type of personality is empirically inclined and prefers facts that can be validated with the senses.[126] Huston Smith states that Jung based his four-function typology of thinking, feeling, sensing, and intuition on this model from Hinduism.

In a similar manner, the Buddha described four main personality types. First were people who had tendencies toward anger and hate. Second were those who were very excitable, lustful, and lost in their own impulsive reactions to events. Third were those who were intellectual and less emotional. Fourth were people who were prone to devotion and religious faith.[127] It is interesting to note that these four types seem to describe primarily which emotions people choose to use when they relate to the world: anger, lust, intellectually controlled emotions, and religious devotion. Tibetan Buddhism iconography often depicts six basic realms of existence that are similar to these personality types. They are called the *Deva-Loka*, or the Six Realms of Rebirth (these will be discussed later in the chapter). However, Jack Kornfield notes that there are a number of different descriptions of personality types in Eastern psychology.[128] Gurus and yoga masters will often assign different spiritual practices based on an analysis of the predominant personality in the student.

PERSONALITY THEORY IN HINDUISM

The Five Sheaths Personality theory in Hinduism begins with the five *kosas*, or "sheaths," which are elements of the three bodies: gross, subtle, and causal. In Vedanta philosophy, the Self, or the ultimate reality that exists in each person, is hidden, in part because it is "covered" or "wrapped" in the *kosas* (figure 3.1).[129]

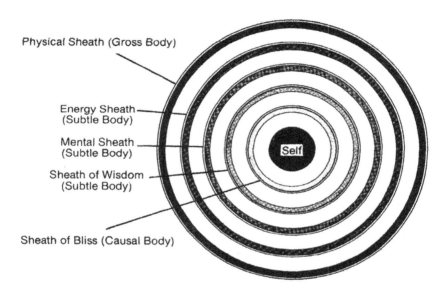

Figure 3.1: The Five Kosas. From the book The Seven Systems of Eastern Philosophy by Pandit Rajmani Tigunait, copyright ©, 1983 by the Himalayan International Institute of Yoga Science and Philosophy of the U.S. A. Reprinted with permission of Himalayan Institute Press.

The Gross Body The outermost, or first, *kosa* is the Gross Body, or the *physical sheath*. This sheath is composed of the physical parts of the body such as the organs, bones, blood, and skin.

The Subtle Body Beneath the physical sheath are the three sheaths of the Subtle Body: the energy, mental, and wisdom sheaths.

The second *kosa*, or the *Energy sheath*, is the first sheath of the Subtle body and is primarily associated with the flow of *prajna* (prah-j-nah) energy in the body. In Hinduism, prajna energy is seen as the life force or primal energy of the universe. The flow of prajna energy is directly connected to the flow of breath in the body. In fact, the regulation of prajna by working with the breath is central to spiritual development (see "Yoga" below).

The third *kosa,* and the second sheath of the Subtle Body, is the *Mental sheath,* or mind. This sheath is a combination of the four instruments of cognition: lower mind, ego, intellect, and mind-stuff. The lower mind (*manas*) is responsible for transferring sensations and emotions from the external to the internal world. The ego (*ahankara*) is that part of us responsible for creating the experience of ourselves as a separate being (see discussion of *asmita* earlier). This element of personality relates to the external world by creating desires for objects and sensations as well as aversions toward unwanted experiences and sensations. The ego works through an internal dynamic created by the two drives of love and hate (or grasping and recoil). It is worth noting that this same dynamic is central to many personality theories in Western psychology. Freud's id drives for sex and aggression are only the most familiar of these perspectives. The intellect (*buddhi*) is the decision-making quality of mind or the rational problem solver. Mind-stuff (*citta*) is the aspect that processes and stores memories that can be recalled later. Rajmani Tigunait has compared the above classification system to Western personality theories and noted that the lower mind, ego, and intellect are essentially the conscious mind in Western psychology, while mind-stuff is the unconscious.[130]

The fourth *kosa,* and the third sheath of the Subtle Body, is the *Wisdom sheath.* This sheath is responsible for transmitting spiritual knowledge from the ultimate reality, or the transcendent Self, to the intellect.

The Causal Body The fifth, and innermost, *kosa* is the causal body, or the *Sheath of Bliss and Perfect Joy.* Since this sheath is very close to the transcendent Self, it can be associated with experiences of joy, bliss, and ecstasy. However, these experiences are still tainted with elements of ego.

The Transcendent Self Finally, the transcendent Self, or the ultimate reality within, lies at the center of the sheaths and energizes the whole process.

Perception and the Five Sheaths The psychological processes involved in sensation, recognition, evaluation, and action can be understood through the interactions among the five sheaths. The process begins with a sense organ of the physical sheath registering a sensation in the external world (e.g., we see a bowl of fresh chocolate ice cream). Next, the experience is transmitted to the lower mind, which makes an initial determination of peril (e.g., not a threat, therefore, no fight-or-flight response is required). The ego then analyzes the experience and creates either aversion or desire (e.g., chocolate ice cream is very, very good!). The perception is then transmitted to the intellect, which then makes a final determination about potential action (e.g., eat the chocolate ice cream!). Every part of this process also leaves an impression in the unconscious, which helps create the seeds of future actions. In the example used here, some of the seeds might be: "desires are good and should be indulged" or "you have no will power and deserve to feel guilty."

If the person identifies with only these psychological processes, then she or he may become a victim of hedonism and fails to realize that the transcendent Self lies hidden beneath, and the person remains trapped by the wheel of karma. If the person is fully enlightened, then he or she may enjoy the chocolate ice cream as one of life's many pleasures, while not creating future karma with unnecessary grasping for similar experiences in the future.

Instincts, Emotions, and Moods Yoga psychology makes distinctions among instincts, emotions, moods, and sentiments.[131] Instincts are involuntary promptings that result in actions. The two most basic instincts are self-preservation and reproduction. Related to the instincts are the three basic impulses: thought, speech, and action. As in contemporary Western psychology, emotions are seen as combinations of desires and thoughts. That is, our emotions are created by our wants and needs plus our cognitive evaluations of experiences. Sentiments are more complex combinations of more basic emotions. The most important for spiritual practices are the religious, aesthetic, and moral sentiments. Moods are enduring combinations of emotions and sentiments. The two most important moods are joy (or exhilaration) and grief (or depression). In general, however, most moods are problematic for spiritual practice, because they trap our minds in one preoccupation after another. In contrast, the moods that are most beneficial to spiritual development include the meditative and devotional (*bhava*).

The Chakra System One of the central concepts in yoga, as well as tantra, concerns the *nadis* and *chakras,* which are the major energy centers of the body. The nadis are subtle energy channels of the body that are roughly coextensive with the nervous system. The chakras are centers of energy in the subtle body that lie roughly along the spinal column. Georg Feuerstein describes the chakras as "psycho-energetic centers" of the body.[132] They are associated with a variety of psychological characteristics, including specific emotions. When the charkas are activated, they will produce specific states of consciousness.

The energy that can activate these centers is called *kundalini* (koon-da-lee-nee). The spiritual practices of kundalini yoga and tantra are focused on releasing and channeling this innate source of energy for spiritual development. For the majority of people, their lower chakras are more active, and, therefore, most people function primarily out of the lower chakras.

The main chakra system is composed of three channels: two channels that wind around the spine roughly in a spiral fashion (often symbolically depicted as a snake or serpent) and a central channel that parallels the spine (figure 3.2). The two channels that wind around the central channel allow prajna energy to flow in the body. The central channel along the spine is composed of the seven chakras and is the major conduit for kundalini energy.[133]

figure 3.2: The Chakra system, from Alchemy: Science of the Cosmos, Science of the Soul by Titus Burkhardt, copyright © 1997, Fons Vitae Publishing. Used with permission.

In most people, the central channel is almost dormant because most kundalini energy is confined to the lower chakras. As spiritual practices bring more energy into the central channel, the kundalini energy combines with prajna energy and can produce an extraordinary burst of kundalini energy, which rushes up toward the highest chakra. As the kundalini activates the chakras, various levels of spiritual illumination are experienced. Some reports of kundalini awakenings are very dramatic and suggest an extraordinarily powerful emotional and spiritual experience. Swami Muktananda described a few of his kundalini awakenings in the following way:[134]

I sometimes danced, sometimes swayed, and sometimes became lost in the love-inspiring nada (cosmic melody). The nada is indeed the Absolute reality...Thus while hearing nada, my mind would converge on its source. I witness the center which, activated by nada, emits divine sparks. All my senses were drawn toward it...My body responded to whatever variety of nada I heard with a corresponding quiver that was mildly painful. Sweating profusely, I felt that I would collapse. My head trembled violently. I felt as if a gentle fire was burning in my body.

It is very important to note that kundalini experiences in a person who is physically and mentally unprepared can be dangerous—especially to one's mental stability. Many of the various techniques of mental discipline, physical conditioning, and bodily cleansing in tantric yoga are meant to prepare the body and mind for the shock of kundalini release and subsequent awakening.

The Seven Chakras The first chakra (*Muladhara*: the base) is located at the base of the spine. It is the source of the dormant kundalini energy. Psychologically, it is often associated with issues of survival and safety. The second chakra (*Swadhisthana*: the sacral) is located approximately several inches above the first. Psychologically, it is a level of consciousness often concerned with addiction to pleasurable experiences, such as sexuality and the differences between men and women. The third chakra (*Manipura*: the solar plexus) is located around the area of the navel and is associated with issues of power, mastery, and the control of impulses.

When the fourth chakra (*Anahata*), at approximately the level of the heart, is activated, there is a tremendous release of positive emotion, especially compassion, altruistic concern, love, and empathy. Swami Ajaya notes that the "transition from the third to fourth chakra is the first step toward the transcendental state, the transcendence of the ego."[135] The fifth chakra (*Vishudda*: the throat) is located around the throat; when activated, it brings a level of consciousness focused on creativity, devotion, and receptivity. The sixth chakra (*Ajna*), located between the eyes, has been called the "third eye," and, in fact, is associated with wisdom, seeing life with a wider perspective, and intuitive knowledge.

Finally, the top of the head is the *Sahasrara* or Crown chakra, the center for profound spiritual consciousness. It is often called the "thousand-petal lotus." At this level of consciousness, all psychological distinctions between dualities dissolve, and a sense of oneness with the universe pervades consciousness. The experience is called *Samadhi* (sah-MAH-dee), or "to put together." What is put together into one unity is the previous duality of self and other.

Georg Feuerstein notes that in traditional yoga, the kundalini energy is seen as "a supremely intelligent power that is the energy aspect of ultimate reality. It is, in itself, super-conscious." He describes kundalini awakening as follows: "When this cosmic intelligent energy reaches the topmost psycho-energetic center at the crown of the head, then practitioners…enter a condition of formless ecstasy and realize the flawless unity of all beings and all things."[136] Each time the kundalini is raised through the chakras, the person's body is slightly transformed. As the process of raising and lowering kundalini is repeated over time, the person's normal physical body is transformed into what is known as the "diamond body," which is a more spiritually mature receptacle for the kundalini energy.

PERSONALITY THEORY IN BUDDHISM

Buddhist personality theory took a somewhat different focus than both the Vedanta and yoga psychologies of the sixth and fifth centuries BCE. First, Buddhism was less concerned with the physical body, because it did not view it as being a "shell" that trapped the transcendental Self. Therefore, the body was not necessarily a hindrance to spiritual development. The Buddha proposed what he called the Middle Way, or a middle path between asceticism and sensory indulgence. Therefore, a healthy physical body was used as a launching pad for spiritual practice.[137] Buddhism was also somewhat less deterministic about the effects of past karma on the process of spiritual liberation. In Buddhism, many expositions of personality theory focus almost exclusively on current psychological process and the creation of a sense of self-identity.

The Five Skandhas Perspectives on personality in Buddhism go into considerable detail concerning what creates the sense of self-identity on a moment-to-moment basis throughout our lives. The building blocks of our sense of self-identity are called the *five skandhas* (skahn-dahs; *khandhas* (P)), the five "heaps," or the five "aggregates."[138] These five building blocks, along with their component parts, are seen as a dynamic system that is in continuous flux. Each element depends on the others to create a stable sense of self-identity, or the internal sense of "I." In spite of the dynamic quality, the development of ego is described as a five-step process. This is partly because the practice of meditation is used to dissolve the illusion of a permanent self in a step-by-step fashion by observing the fundamental unreality of each part of this process.

The five skandhas are categorized into two divisions. The first skandha is associated with the body, whereas the other four skandhas are associated with the mind. These last four skandhas are collectively known as *nama,* or the *psyche.* It is interesting to note the similarities between the five skandhas of Buddhism and the five kosas of Hinduism.

The First Skandha: Form, or the body Development of a sense of self begins with the physical body. At this point in the development of self-identity, what has developed is knowledge of the body and sense organs. It is a fundamental starting point for the creation of an experiencing self.

The Second Skandha: Sensations, or feelings At this step, sensations and sensory experiences are separated into pleasant, unpleasant, and neutral. However, these categorizations are still very primitive. In fact, they are not considered emotions at this point, because emotions are more complex combinations of cognitive and physiological elements. The sensations and feelings at this point have more to do with innate attractions or repulsions to certain stimuli. It should be noted that in Eastern psychology, the senses include the usual five of sight, sound, taste, smell, and touch, along with the mind as a sixth sense.

The Third Skandha: Perception At this point, stimuli are recognized and formed into coherent concepts or categories. We also begin to make judgments about how to react to those conceptualizations. Our reactions at this point, however, are quite automatic and occur before any reflection. In Buddhist personality theory, we develop three basic strategies for relating to the perceptions we form. These three are (1) aggression, hatred, or anger (symbolized by a snake); (2) desire, greed, or craving (symbolized by a rooster); and (3) ignorance, stupidity, delusion, or defensive indifference (symbolized by a pig). Some descriptions of Buddhist personality types list these three as the basic types.[139]

In the Tibetan Buddhist Wheel of Life, these three occupy the center of the wheel, with each chasing the other (figures 3.3 and 3.4). In other words, these three are our most fundamental reactions to stimuli. Further, if we do not take steps to control them in some way, they will drive our behavior compulsively throughout life. Once again, note that in some Western personality theories, these three are also given a central role. Again, the best-known example comes from Freud, who spoke of aggression and sex as fundamental drives and also believed that defense mechanisms were a fundamental part of personality.

The Fourth Skandha: Mental acts, mental forms, volition, will At this point, we have the capacity to deliberately choose how to react to stimuli. We can categorize and name experience in complex ways as well as speculate about or interpret events. The most important mental formation is the creation of self-identity, an internal self-representation, or the sense of "I." All of the necessary elements for a sense of self are now present, and the sense of I-am-ness can be created from the mixture. In addition, as at this point we can make volitional choices, future karma can now be created, because only our willful acts can create our karma.

The Fifth Skandha: Consciousness In Buddhism, consciousness is understood as the psychological function that coordinates all the other elements. Chogyam Trungpa says that at this point, the basic materials of the body, our sensations, the orienting responses of our perceptions, our active will, and our intellectualizations combine to produce our inner world of thoughts and emotions.[140] What we take to be reality is now fully created.

The Yogachara school of Buddhism (or the Mind-Only School) added a sixth element, which they call the foundation or store-consciousness (*alaya-vijnana*). This is an unconscious element that contains healthy and unhealthy "seeds," which are created by actions. As the path of meditation progresses, one consequence is that healthy seeds replace the unhealthy seeds. Interestingly, the store-consciousness is both individual and collective. It has been suggested that the store-consciousness is similar to Jung's idea of a collective unconscious (also see the above discussions of *sanchita karma* and *citta*/mind-stuff).[141]

The Six Realms Once consciousness creates our sense of reality, there follows a tendency for many people to maintain consistency to their own self-created inner world. These internal consistencies often result in outward behavioral consistencies. In Western psychology, these consistencies have been called *personality types*. In Tibetan Buddhism, the six basic personality types are termed the *Deva-Loka*, or the Six Realms of Rebirth.[142] Note that these are not exactly Western-style personality traits such as openness to experience or neuroticism. In the West, personality traits describe primarily behavioral and emotional consistencies over time and secondarily consistencies in how information is processed psychologically. In the six realms, these emphases are reversed, so that consistencies of psychological processing are primary and behavioral consistencies are secondary. Therefore, the six realms are clusters of related psychological states that determine how we consistently view reality. They may also describe the basic types of psychological experience that we create throughout the day. That is, we may experience many of these styles of consciousness during a typical day, and each describes our outlook on the world and ourselves at that moment in time. In the Wheel of Life, the six realms are each depicted metaphorically and symbolically in a circle that immediately surrounds the rooster, the pig, and the snake at the center (see figure 3.4).

figure 3.3: Tibetan Buddhist Wheel of Life.

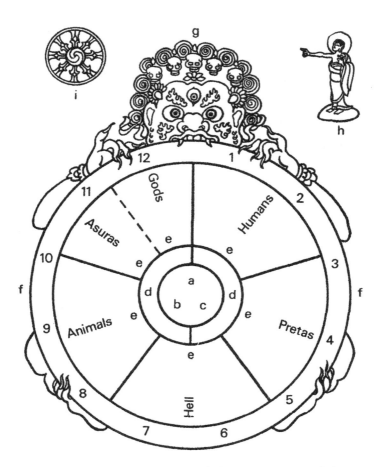

figure 3.4: Images in the Wheel of Life: (a.) cock - craving, (b.) snake - greed, (c.) pig - ignorance, (d.) happy & sad people —the cycle of life, (e.) six realms of existence,(f. #1 - #12) 12 links in the chain of dependent origination, (g.) Yama the Lord of Death who rules the cycle of birth & death, (h.) the Buddha pointing beyond the Wheel of Life toward (i.) Asoka's Wheel - symbol of the Dharma, the Doctrine of the Buddha, the Universal law. From The Tantric Mysticism of Tibet by John Blofeld, copyright © 1970, George Allen and Unwin Ltd. Used by permission of Dutton, a division of Penguin Group (USA), Inc.

The Three Lower Realms The three lower realms on the Wheel of Life refer to realms where rebirths result from evil acts. The lowest is the *Hell* realm (recall the discussion of hell in chapter 2). From a psychological point of view, the hell realm is defined as a mental state controlled and dominated by anger and aggression. Everything in the world seems hostile, unwelcoming, and dangerous.[143]

The next lowest is the realm of the *Hungry Ghosts*, or *Pretas*. These are beings that are tormented by unending and insatiable desires. Psychologically, we exist in the realm of the hungry ghosts when we desperately crave what we do not have. People who are driven by desires for money, power, excitement, or sensual pleasures are caught in the realm of the hungry ghosts. To get a feel for this realm, just remember the last time that you passionately and desperately wanted something. You could have wanted a new car, a new career, or a special person in your life, but remember how consumed you were by that desire. Obviously, people caught by materialism or consumerism are stuck in this realm. Interestingly, from a Buddhist perspective, any society based on materialistic consumerism is founded on the idea that everyone needs to be trapped in the realm of the hungry ghosts for the society to operate efficiently.

The next lowest is the *Animal* realm. From a symbolic standpoint, in this realm we are reborn as animals and must suffer the indignities and cruelties that animals suffer. Psychologically, this realm describes a personality style in which people go through life in an unreflective and automatic manner. They never question the rules they live by, or they never venture outside the boundaries of the known and predictable. Behavior is quite instinctual and without intellectual reflection. In this realm, people can be very stubborn, self-absorbed, and focused on comfort and convenience.

The Three Upper Realms The upper three realms of the circle are the result of good karma. The lowest of these is the *Human* realm, and in terms of human motivation, it is the most important. From this realm, people can take actions that will increase good karma and facilitate their progress toward enlightenment and release from the cycle of rebirth. From a psychological perspective, the human realm involves a passionate pursuit of higher ideals. When in this realm, we are involved in learning, expanding potentials, and developing talents. It is a very intellectual realm, with much effort put into discursive thought. Although this may sound interesting and even compelling, we are also quite ambitious in this realm. This makes us very busy, always searching for new challenges and new ways of thinking about the world. The constant drive for new adventures, challenges, and new ways to reinvent ourselves creates an underlying tension that cannot be erased. Note that most Western theories of mental health would view this realm as the goal of healthy personality development. In the West, this passionate, involved, and committed sense of goal-directed behavior is seen as the ideal model for good mental health. From a Buddhist perspective, Western psychology urges all of us to strive toward life in the human realm.

The next realm is that of the *Asuras*, which is also referred to as the realm of the *Jealous Gods*, *Demigods*, *Titans*, or *anti-god*. The personality characteristics associated with this realm come from feeling that you have achieved something very special. Therefore, this realm gives a sense of self-satisfaction, self-importance, and pride. It is a realm where we bask in our own self-importance. Although these emotions may be seen as pleasant, what goes hand-in-hand with this is worrying that something or someone will intrude and will take these emotions away from you. What results is a feeling of competitiveness, worry, envy, and paranoia, along with a sense that you can't trust others, as well as a constant need to compare yourself with others to see if you are still worthy of respect and admiration.

The last realm, at the top of the circle, is the realm of the *Gods*, the *Deva realm*, or the *realm of bliss*. This is one of the trickiest realms, because it initially appears very desirable and filled with splendid experiences. In fact, many Buddhist texts refer to this as the *Heaven* realm. As an example, Trungpa's description of this realm focuses on someone who has achieved prowess with meditation. He says that in this realm, meditators have been able to enter absorptive states and experience heavenly visions and blissful altered states. However, they become addicted to these ecstatic states and use them to feed their own self-identity. In essence, they congratulate themselves for the extraordinary spiritual experiences they have achieved. However, if we are in this realm, we are aware at some level that the blissful states we can produce during meditation will all fade. Therefore, we are forced into seeking them again, rather than finding a way to accept all of life as it is. In the realm of the Gods, we can collect spiritual experiences to feed our sense of self-importance and fall victim to what Trungpa calls "spiritual materialism."[144]

Summary of the Six Realms To summarize the six realms, they describe personality styles that we habitually use to protect ourselves from worry, fear, and doubt, as well as to enhance our sense of self-importance and accomplishment. While many people in the East take them literally as realms of rebirth, they may also be seen psychologically. The realms may be interpreted as a list of basic personality traits or as typical states of consciousness that we experience repeatedly on a day-to-day basis.

That is, on any day we can feel negative emotions, such as feeling trapped, hopeless, and guilty (hell realm); we can experience envy, craving, and a need to fill ourselves up with experiences (hungry ghosts); or we may remain resistant, rigid, overly intellectual, and unreflective to protect ourselves (animal realm). When we feel happy during the same day, we can alternate between joy over what we have acquired and worry that it won't last (jealous gods); we can bask in our own accomplishments (realm of the gods, heaven); or we can pursue our own personal dreams and passions in the hopes of finding greater self-esteem, self-actualization, or flourishing (human realm).

From the perspective of Buddhist personality theory, although some of these states are very pleasurable, each of these describes a way by which we remain trapped in cycles that produce unhappiness and suffering. The purpose of meditation practice is to help us transcend these ways of solidifying our self-reflective identity and find a truly lasting peace of mind.

Dependent Origination In Buddhist personality theory, the whole chain of events that creates our personal self-concept and maintains our entrapment in continuous rebirths is termed *dependent origination*, dependent co-arising, conditioned genesis, or the chain of causation *(paticca-samuppada* in Pali*)*. This is the Buddhist law of moral cause and effect; it expresses how suffering is created and how it can be stopped.[145] The idea is usually expressed as a sequence of twelve steps. Each step will lead inevitably to the next, unless the process is interrupted by disciplined meditation practice. The following presentation of dependent origination is taken from Walpola Rahula:[146]

(1) Ignorance of the Four Noble Truths (see chapters 2 and 4)

(2) Ignorance conditions the karmic consequences of volitional actions

(3) Volitional actions condition our consciousness

(4) Consciousness conditions how we create mental and physical phenomenon

(5) Phenomena condition the six faculties (i.e., five senses and mind)

(6) Six faculties condition sensory and mental content

(7) Sensory and mental content condition sensation

(8) Sensation conditions desire

(9) Desire conditions clinging

(10) Clinging conditions the process of becoming

(11) Becoming conditions birth

(12) Birth conditions death and rebirth

Rahula cautions us to remember that these twelve steps are actually all aspects of an interdependent, dynamic process. Everything in life is conditioned, relative, and interdependent. He calls it the "Buddhist theory of relativity" and states, "It should clearly be remembered that each of these factors is conditioned as well as conditioning. Therefore they are all relative, interdependent and interconnected, and nothing is absolute or independent; hence no first cause is accepted in Buddhism."[147] In keeping with this idea, in the Wheel of Life, these steps are seen as a circle—the outer circle of the Wheel of Life that encompasses all the other processes (figure 3.4).

The theory of dependent origination is also seen as supplying the rationale for the Buddhist idea of *anatta* (ah-na-ta), or the doctrine that there is no permanent self and no immortal soul. As everything is conditioned, dynamic, and interdependent, there is no permanent entity that can be found that exists outside of the constantly changing conditions. Our entire psychological life can be seen in terms of always changing, interdependent transactions among the psychological elements that make up our sense of self.

TAOIST PERSONALITY THEORY

In Taoism the descriptions of personality are placed in language that is far more metaphorical and poetic. In fact, Taoist descriptions of the human personality and energy systems of the body can be quite baffling to readers trained in Western styles of explanation. To complicate matters even further, Chinese ideas on human behavior include influences from forces in nature and celestial bodies. For instance, Taoists believe that yin and yang were originally combined within the Tao, forming the "primordial breath."[148] When these two separated, they formed heaven and earth, which later separated into humans and all other creatures. In this way, humans are formed of heavenly and earthly "breaths." Using language that is even more metaphorical and symbolic, the process of psychological transformation is described with alchemical images, such as using "fire" to heat "cauldrons" in which "precious metals" such as "gold" are processed and transformed.

As stated earlier, the concept of personality traits in Western psychology refers to enduring patterns of behavior recognized over time and over various situations. In general, Taoists would consider these consistencies in behavior to be signs of imbalance, psychological rigidity, and poor mental health. Logically, if the Tao is the fundamental dynamic energy of the universe, and the idea of mental health is to allow the Tao to guide one's actions, then overly consistent patterns of behavior tend to indicate a resistance to change, spontaneity, and the Tao. Nonetheless, it is recognized that most people exhibit certain regularities of behavior.

The Three Basic Energies In Taoism it is believed that at birth, we have three basic energies that propel existence: *chi* (qi), or vital energy; *ching* (jing), or generative energy; and *shen,* or spirit energy. Chi is the energy of the universe. Ching is the combination of chi from both parents and provides for our temperament and personality characteristics.[149] Shen is consciousness, or what makes us uniquely human. It is also responsible for spiritual insights and enlightenment. Unfortunately, as we age, these can dissipate, which leads to ill health, old age, and death. It is through the process of spiritual training or inner alchemy that the energy we have been given can be directed and either retained or recovered.

The Five Major Elements Another major aspect of Taoist personality theory is the idea of the five elements: earth, fire, water, wood, and metal. These are the fundamental divisions of the cosmos out of which all elements of existence are created. Each element is related to a specific season, climate, cardinal direction, color, sense organ, organ of the body, and emotion.[150] For example, the following emotions are associated with the five elements: pensiveness with earth, joy with fire, fear or fright with water, anger with wood, and sadness or grief with metal. It deserves mentioning at this point that the Chinese do not rigidly categorize emotions, and overlaps among different emotions are considered normal.

According to Taoist thought, these five elements and seven emotions are in a constant state of dynamic interrelationship. The image of the t'ai-chi symbol with its interpenetrating polarities represents this dynamic relationship. When they are balanced, energy flows in harmony with the Tao. When out of balance, problems are created in the individual and in society. Although every element is related to the others, there are lines of major influence among the elements.

Patterns of emotional balance and imbalance are also associated with the five elements. When earth is balanced, this enhances concentration, patience, creative thinking, and mental stability. When earth is out of balance, this can lead to obsessive behavior and distractions. When fire is in balance, this leads to spontaneity, resilience, curiosity, and a sense of fulfillment in life. A lack of joy and a loss of personal boundaries can result when fire is out of balance. When water is balanced, a person can remain poised and calm in spite of his or her circumstances. When water is out of balance, one lacks goals and a sense of direction. A balance of wood allows one to transcend limitations and set worthy goals. Unbalanced wood can lead to depression, impulsiveness, anger, or inertia. Finally, balanced metal supports disciplined reflection, learning from experience, and self-respect. Unbalanced metal can lead to low self-esteem, regret, and being trapped by memories of one's past.

As mentioned, another one of the many difficulties with understanding Taoist personality theory from a Western point of view is that Taoism assumes human behavior can be strongly influenced by forces in the natural world. That is, as humans are an intimate part of the natural world, forces in nature may affect human emotions and behavior. A familiar example in the West is the art of *feng-shui*, which attempts to create harmony between people, dwellings, and the invisible forces of the natural world. In fact, in many ways the contributions of any individual to his or her behavior are secondary to the causal influences from the holistic and dynamic pattern of interactions among all forces in the system: natural, social, physiological, psychological, and spiritual.

The Major Energy Channels of the Body Taoists believe that there are three major channels for energy in the human body (figure 3.5). Interestingly, the system is remarkably similar to the chakra system of yoga. The first channel is the *Microcosmic Orbit*, which is a channel that begins at the base of the spine, travels up the spine to the top of the head, then down the front of the body and back to the base of the spine. It is composed of two meridians. The *tu mo* meridian travels from the base of the spine over the head and ends at the upper palate inside the mouth. This also called the *governor channel*, or channel of control, and it is associated with yang energy, or the ascent of positive fire. The *jen mo* meridian begins at the lower mouth and travels down the front of the body to the base of the spine.[151] This is also known as the *functional channel*, and it is associated with yin energy, or the descent of negative fire.

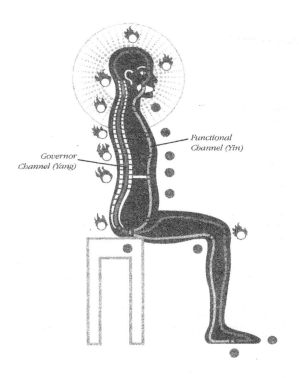

Governor Channel (Yang)

Functional Channel (Yin)

figure 3.5: Taoist Energy Channels, from The Essence of Tao by Pamela Ball, copyright © 2004, Arcturus Publications/Eagle editions, London. Used with permission.

The second channel is the *Macrocosmic Orbit,* which consists of the Microcosmic orbit plus an energy channel that travels down the legs to the soles of the feet and back. Energy can flow in either direction in the macrocosmic orbit. In addition to these two channels, there is a third, called the *thrusting channel,* or *ch'ung mo.* It moves through the center of the body, connecting the brain and the base of the torso.

Meditative practices help move these energies through the channels of the microcosmic orbit. The regulation of the breath is especially important to this process. Many meditation practices will advise practitioners to place their tongue gently on the roof of their mouth during meditation. Taoists believe this action connects the two major meridians of the microcosmic orbit.

The Three Tan-t'iens (or dan tiens) In Taoist personality theory, the spiritual centers of the body are described using metaphors of alchemy. The process of refining and transforming the energies of the body is expressed as igniting the internal "fires" in various "cauldrons." The processes necessary for moving the refined energies through the body are controlled by meditation practices. The spiritual energy system is divided into three major *tan-t'iens,* or cauldrons.[152] Each tan-t'ien is controlled by a "gate" that can be found along the spinal column.

The First Tan-t'ien: the lower cauldron The gate associated with this tan-t'ien is located along the spinal column in the area of the kidneys. It is found in roughly the same place as the *manipura chakra* of kundalini yoga (see description of the chakras above). Opening the gate of the lower tan-t'ien allows the three energies to be gathered for the initial refinement and transmutation. In the lower tan-t'ien around the area of the navel is the major "furnace," which ignites the fires for transmutation of generative energy (*ching*) into what is called the *alchemical agent.*

The Second Tan-t'ien: the middle cauldron The gate is found along the spine between the shoulder blades, or around the area of the *anahata chakra.* It is in this area that the alchemical agent is gathered and refined into vital energy (*chi*).

The Third Tan-t'ien: the upper cauldron Its gate is located where the spine enters the base of the skull. This is roughly between the *vishuddha* and *ajna* charkas of kundalini yoga. This tan-t'ien is associated with the transmutation of vital energy into spirit energy (*shen*).

The Golden Flower The final product of refining and transmuting the three energies is referred to as the "Golden Flower," or the "Golden Elixer."[153] The emergence of the Golden Flower is referred to as the Three Flowers Gathering at the top of the head. In kundalini yoga, the top of the head is referred to as the *sahasrara* (thousand-petaled) or crown chakra. It is interesting to note that both the Taoist and kundalini systems use the metaphor of a flower for this energy center of the body.

The incredible similarity between the Taoist system and the kundalini system can only be explained in two ways. Either there was cross-cultural contact, or it represents independent emergence. There was certainly cross-cultural contact between India and China in the early years of Taoism. In fact, it would appear that many of the ideas of Chinese yoga were in fact imported from India.[154] However, the Taoist system today is considerably different from Indian yoga. For instance, Taoist yoga assumes the energy of the human body is oriented to the four cardinal points (north, south, east, and west), which in turn is related to the magnetic fields of the planet. In addition, a number of further divisions of the energy system are also present, such as the twelve subdivisions of the microcosmic orbit.[155]

LEVELS OF CONSCIOUSNESS IN EASTERN PSYCHOLOGY

Many theories of psychology will propose a series of recognizable changes that people go through as personality development proceeds. These changes may be common changes seen over time, as in child and adult development, or they may be more uncommon changes in personality as a result of psychological growth, such as self-actualization. The Eastern perspectives on mental health and personality development all postulate a series of steps or stages that a person will go through as he or she develops and refines meditation skills. These steps describe the recognizable changes in consciousness and awareness that people will experience as they move toward samadhi, enlightenment, or the merging with the Tao. The levels of awareness presented below are the most general formulation. More specific descriptions of these levels are associated with meditation practice and will be presented in the next chapter.

VEDIC PSYCHOLOGY

Maharishi Mahesh Yogi, the founder of transcendental meditation, describes the seven major states of consciousness that are discussed in Vedic psychology.[156] The first three states are waking consciousness, sleeping, and dreaming. As mentioned before, these are also recognized by Western psychology. The next four states are true altered states of awareness and are hierarchically arranged levels of consciousness. The fourth state is transcendental consciousness. At this level, active processes of thought are quieted, resulting in a deep serenity. Ordinary perception is altered, so that "knower, known, and the process of knowing converge in one unbroken field of awareness free of all content." The fifth state is cosmic consciousness. At this level, awareness is no longer tied to the personal identity or sense of self. Instead, awareness is centered in the transcendent Self, or atman. The sixth state is refined cosmic consciousness. At this point, the identification of the limited or personal self with the higher Self is expanded to begin a unification of the Self with the universal reality, or Brahman. As the awareness of the sixth state is further refined, the seventh state of unity consciousness is experienced. Now the subtle separation between Self and the universal activity of Brahman disappears. Emotionally, this experience results in an overwhelming sense of unity or oneness and an experience of universal love.

RAM DAS ON THE LEVELS OF CONSCIOUSNESS

Ram Das is a Western psychologist who left traditional psychology to pursue a full-time spiritual path under the guidance of an Indian guru. For over forty years, he has been a bridge between Western and Eastern models of mental health. His description of the levels of self-awareness involves five levels.[157] He uses the metaphor of changing channels on a TV set to describe movement through the levels. The first level involves identification with one's physical body. Self-identity at this level is defined by how one looks or appears to others. The second level is associated with one's "psycho-social identity." The identification at this level is with one's personality. The third level involves identification with universal and cross-cultural themes and images. Ram Das says this level involves the collective unconscious and archetypes, as described by Jung. It is the last level discussed in any traditional Western personality theory. The fourth level is a level of awareness where a person experiences a feeling of oneness with the universe. The fifth, and last, level is a level of awareness that transcends all dualities. It is beyond the concepts of time and space. Hinduism calls it a merging with Brahman, Buddhists refer to it as sunyata, or emptiness; Taoists call it flowing with the Tao; and Christian contemplatives say it is a merging with God.

THE TEN OX HEARDING PICTURES OF ZEN

The *Ten Ox Herding Pictures* of Zen provide another interesting perspective on the stages of spiritual development.[158] In these pictures, the ox symbolizes a person's Buddha-nature, or the innate connection to ultimate reality. The first six pictures involve the following stages: beginning a search for one's Buddha-nature (i.e., Truth), seeing the first glimpses of Buddha-nature, becoming adept at experiencing Buddha-nature, and allowing Buddha-nature to permeate one's life. The last four pictures, however, represent finer distinctions within the last stages of spiritual training. In picture 7, the distinction between secular and sacred is transcended—everything in life is seen as sacred. In picture 8, even the distinction between enlightenment and nonenlightenment is transcended. Picture 9 symbolizes the realization that all of life, exactly as it presents itself in every moment, is a perfect reflection of the highest universal Truth. Finally, picture 10 shows the person—who is now a bodhisattva—returning to the normal world to help other people through spiritual teachings or simply by his or her presence. The monk or the nun now lives in the world with ultimate compassion, joy, and equanimity.

CLOSING THOUGHTS

This chapter has very briefly covered the ideas of Hinduism, Buddhism, and Taoism on the structure of the human personality. These ideas range from Buddhist descriptions of the self, which are vaguely reminiscent of Western psychological descriptions, to the Taoist descriptions that appear at first glance to have nothing whatsoever in common with Western psychology. The descriptions of tantra and the chakra system in Hinduism also postulate processes that are completely foreign to Western psychology. Because of the very obvious divergences from the Western philosophical and scientific tradition, this chapter may have been the most challenging presentation so far. Nevertheless, within their own cultural milieu, these descriptions of internal psychological processes have proven to be very useful tools for many people for thousands of years.

CHAPTER 4

Meditation and Spiritual Practices
In Eastern Psychology

> In Samadhi…just as a river merges into the ocean, so does
> the individual soul merge into the supreme soul—and all
> limitations disappear.
>
> SWAMI RAMA [159]

There is little doubt that the practical techniques developed in Eastern psychology to foster well-being have had the most visible impact on Western societies. Not only are most Westerners familiar with techniques such as yoga, meditation, tai chi chuan, and other martial arts, but many people are also dedicated practitioners of these disciplines. Although these disciplines are prevalent in the West, most Westerners practice them to improve mental health and well-being defined from a Western perspective, rather than for spiritual goals as defined in the East.

To begin this discussion, it should be said that adepts of Eastern psychology recognize that the meditation techniques they devote many hours to each day can also be used for more secular purposes. They recognize that there are numerous degrees of dedication to the spiritual practices that they devote their lives to. An example from Zen may illustrate a loose categorization system that is fairly common in most advanced Eastern psychologies.

Zen master Yasutani-roshi [160] said that there are five basic ways to practice Zen.[161] The first way to practice is focused only on improving mental and physical health. It is meditation, open to anyone, because it is free of philosophical and religious content. The second way to practice Zen does involve a religious element, but the goal is to cultivate special states of consciousness or unique spiritual experiences. While these practices require strenuous and consistent efforts, they are seen as a lesser form of spiritual practice. Yasutani-roshi said that the third way to practice Zen is to set one's goal on experiencing enlightenment only for oneself. Although having enlightenment experiences shows a person a glimpse of ultimate reality, this glimpse is sought after in a somewhat self-centered fashion. Practitioners who are trapped in spiritual materialism would fall into this level (see chapter 3). The fourth way to practice Zen is to view practice as a way to actualize Buddha-nature, or the ultimate reality, in one's life. In this practice style, the goal is not simply to have spiritual experiences, but also to allow the practice of Zen and the experiences that occur to profoundly transform one's thinking, emotions, and behavior. In particular, one's sense of self, or the representational ego, is radically transformed. The fifth, and last, way to practice Zen is one in which the means and the end coalesce—one's everyday life is seen as the most profound expression of the ultimate reality or Buddha-nature. As mentioned before, when eighth-century Chinese Ch'an master P'ang Chu-Shih was asked what he had achieved through meditation, he answered, "How wonderful, how mysterious! I chop wood, I carry water." At this point, there is no struggle for enlightenment, for exotic states of consciousness, or for release from the "burden" of suffering.

When people discuss meditation practice, often the distinctions between these ways of practice are overlooked, and this can cause confusion.[162] Some of the confusion may be understandable, given the fact that many techniques can be useful at any level of spiritual practice. That is, meditation can be used simply for relaxation, and it can also be used to radically alter one's sense of self and one's understanding of the nature of reality.

SPIRITUAL PRACTICES ACROSS THE LIFESPAN

Most schools of Eastern psychology assume that a person can begin training at any point in his or her life. However, in Hinduism, a unique lifespan perspective has evolved. The lifespan is divided into four parts: student, householder, retirement, and renunciate or *sannyasin* (san-yah-seen). During the student stage, a person learns the necessary roles and knowledge of his or her culture. During the householder stage, the person is involved in work, family, and civic duties. Retirement is the opportunity to withdraw from many social obligations. The focus should be on seeking greater truths about life's meaning and the search for wisdom. In the last stage, the person takes up a spiritual practice in earnest. In this stage of life, the person may renounce normal worldly concerns and enter a monastery or ashram in order to focus entirely on spiritual development.

In this lifespan model, it is only after a person has fulfilled his or her obligations to family and society that a completely dedicated spiritual practice is undertaken. Of course, many people choose to begin a serious spiritual practice much earlier in life and forgo career, family, and worldly concerns. Nonetheless, the notion that spiritual practice should be part of everyone's life has been integrated into Indian ideas about developmental life stages.

BASIC FOUNDATIONS OF SPIRITUAL PRACTICES

Generally, the first task of any technique in Eastern psychology is to quiet down the obsessive quality of our usual cognitive and emotional responses. Theoretically, if the incessant chatter of the mind can be quieted down sufficiently, then at that point the underlying connection to the ultimate reality can be realized.

Roger Walsh described what he believed were the seven essential practices of any spiritual discipline.[163] These seven are as follows:

(1) Living ethically

(2) Redirecting motivation

(3) Transforming emotions

(4) Developing concentration

(5) Refining awareness

(6) Cultivating wisdom

(7) Practicing service and generosity

To accomplish these tasks, all Eastern perspectives on spiritual development will take a holistic approach to training. To varying degrees, each perspective on training will emphasize changes in thinking, in emotions, and in behavior. Each also views the body and mind as interconnected. Therefore, most practice styles of Eastern psychology will emphasize all of the following as part of the spiritual training: healthy body, intellectual understanding, the adoption of altruistic behaviors, compassionate motivations, and meditation practices. Of course, the emphasis placed on each of these areas shows considerable variation among the different types of training, but all areas are emphasized to some degree in any formal training.

Formal training in these spiritual disciplines also requires considerable commitment and sacrifice. Often the dedication and effort needed to mature the new consciousness requires the aspirant to temporarily retire to a monastery or a temple in order to completely focus all her or his attention on spiritual training. It is also assumed that the development of the necessary skill and expertise may require many years of practice. Some years ago, European psychiatrist Medard Boss visited a number of monasteries in India. After these visits, he observed, "[C]ompared with the degree of self-purification expected by the [Eastern spiritual practices], even the best Western psychoanalytic training is not much more than an introductory course."[164]

THE GURU OR TEACHER

In Eastern meditative practices, it is usually assumed that a spiritual teacher or guide is necessary to learn and navigate the difficulties of advanced spiritual training. The person beginning training needs someone who has taken the same road before and who knows the difficulties, traps, and pitfalls and possesses a decent map. One term for a spiritual teacher is *guru*, which means "one who dispels the darkness of ignorance."[165] Other terms for the guru or teacher include the Tibetan Buddhist honorifics *lama* and *rinpoche* (RIN-po-shey, an incarnate lama), *sage* in Taoism, and *roshi* (ROW-she) in Zen. In Eastern spiritual practices, a person's relationship with his or her guru can be an extremely intense emotional experience. For example, the practice of bhakti yoga can use feelings of love and devotion to one's guru as an important step in training. In psychoanalytic terms, these relationships can involve intense transference reactions focused on the guru.[166] Obviously, if these intense emotional reactions to one's teacher are not handled properly, they can be a source of emotional difficulty for the student.

MORAL AND ETHICAL BEHAVIOR

Hinduism, Buddhism, and Taoism all begin with the assertion that genuine spiritual attainment is not possible without a foundation of ethical and moral behavior. This is not because unethical and immoral behavior is a sin. In fact, the Judeo-Christian concept of sin is virtually nonexistent in Eastern psychologies.[167] The consequences of immoral behavior are not eternal damnation, but rather finding oneself continuously trapped in the whirlwind cycle of future rebirths and future suffering. However, it is always possible to begin spiritual training and eventually remove oneself from this whirlwind. What leads to immoral behavior is a lack of wisdom and a lack of connection to the ultimate reality, which allows justifications and excuses for one's impulsive and egocentric behavior.

Each strand of Eastern psychology has its own unique list of the basic ethical and moral principles that should be developed. However, there is considerable similarity among the different disciplines. These principles are guidelines that help practitioners develop a spiritual practice to the fullest extent possible. In addition, the Eastern psychologies believe the behavior of someone who is an enlightened guru, arhat, or sage naturally and spontaneously conveys a strong sense of highly developed ethical and moral principles. Therefore, a student might as well begin spiritual training by imitating the behavior of the people he or she wishes to emulate.

MEDITATION

At the core of all Eastern disciplines is the practice of meditation. Meditation is the primary discipline by which consciousness is transformed. In this context, however, meditation is not synonymous with relaxation or philosophical speculation. The term *meditation* in this context refers to a disciplined and dedicated approach to training awareness and concentration. In Hinduism, the word for meditation is *dhyana*, which means "absorption," and often refers to one-pointed concentration. In Buddhism, the word for meditation comes from the word *bhavana*, which can be translated as "mental culture" or "mental development." Deane Shapiro defines meditation as "a family of techniques which have in common a conscious attempt to focus attention in a non-analytic way and an attempt not to dwell on discursive, ruminative thought."[168] In other words, it is a disciplined practice that seeks to focus awareness on the context in which thinking and emotions appear, rather than on the thoughts and emotions themselves.

It should be mentioned that the term *meditation* covers much more than the familiar practice form of sitting on a small cushion. A quick look at the scope of meditation techniques reveals an astounding variety of ways through which people may encourage their own spiritual development. There are styles of meditation that involve sitting, standing, walking, stretching (e.g., yoga), movement (e.g., tai chi chuan), chanting, visualization, artistic expression, and even drinking tea. Note that this list includes both contemplative and active styles of meditation. The active styles of meditation engage the body and stimulate the central nervous system. Examples of this style would include energetic Sufi dancing and martial arts schools, which are grounded in a spiritual approach to life. One of the most intriguing, or perhaps bewildering, practices for many people in the West is the use of sexual activity for spiritual purposes. Given the range of behaviors that can be used as meditation, it is clear that meditation can be practiced literally every moment of the day.

As mentioned earlier, a major objective of meditation is to quiet our ordinary mental activities and allow the underlying spiritual reality to emerge. However, trying to use one's mental processes to stop thinking seems like the familiar challenge to stop thinking about pink elephants. Paradoxically, your effort to stop thinking produces more thoughts. In some sense, the various forms of meditation are each attempts to solve this paradox.

For instance, some forms of meditation give the mind a single object to focus on as a way to build concentration. When awareness is focused on a single object, the ultimate reality may emerge while the mind is focusing in some other direction. Some other forms of meditation will cultivate a calm, yet interested, detachment from the mind's activities. In these styles of meditation, the mind is allowed to operate, but the person slowly trains him- or herself to create a space of awareness that is not tied to the normal activities of the thinking mind. In a common simile used in Zen, this allows the mind to clear like the silt settling to the bottom of a quiet, clear lake. Interestingly, other forms of meditation will try to overpower the normal mind's hold on our awareness. This may be accomplished by dramatic episodes of raising spiritual energy or confounding normal intellectual processes with illogical-sounding riddles or puzzles. Finally, some forms simply advocate doing nothing special. The meditation instruction is to "just sit."

THE PATH OF SPIRITUAL TRAINING

Most systematized methods on how to master meditation skills have developed a set of steps a person takes during his or her training. In practice, of course, all of the training steps are intertwined and complement each other.

YOGA

Yoga is the practical school of philosophy in Indian thought. Patanjali's yoga is also known as *ashtanga* yoga, raja yoga (the "Royal Path"), or the eightfold path.[169] This path consists of eight steps, or limbs (Table 4.1). The first five are known as the external limbs, because they focus on control of moral behavior, of the physical body, and of the senses. The last three limbs are called the internal limbs. As might be guessed, these three are directed at the control of consciousness. The most frequently found yoga in the Western world is hatha yoga, which is described by the first four limbs.

The Eight Limbs of Astanga or Patanjala Yoga

External Limbs:	Hatha Yoga
1. Moral Discipline (Yamas)	1.
2. Self-restraint (Niyamas)	2.
3. Postures (Asanas)	3.
4. Control of Prajna (Pranayama)	4.
5. Sensory Inhibition (Pratyahara)	
Internal Limbs:	
6. Concentration (Dharana)	
7. Meditation (Dhyana)	
8. Spiritual Absorption (Samadhi)	

Table 4.1: The Eight Limbs of Astanga or Patanjala Yoga

The first two limbs constitute the moral code of yoga. The first limb is *Moral Discipline,* or the *Yamas.* There are five principles of moral discipline: non-harming, truthfulness, non-stealing, chastity, and non-grasping.[170] These five are meant to help harmonize interpersonal relationships. Practicing non-harming refers to not creating physical or mental harm to others, and it helps overcome anger. Truthfulness refers to being honest and showing integrity in dealings with others. This helps overcome delusion or ignorance. Non-stealing helps overcome greed. Chastity is not the same idea as celibacy, but rather refers to maintaining control over sexuality. Chastity helps us overcome uncontrolled desires and passions. In yoga it is not always necessary to suppress or even repress sexuality. Instead, we should express sexuality in an appropriate manner, so we don't become obsessively attached to it. Non-grasping is to "abstain from actively cluttering up our lives with material and intellectual things...but to let go of them." It helps overcome acquisitiveness and greed.

There are also five principles associated with the second limb of *Self-Restraint,* or the *Niyamas*: purity, contentment, austerity, self-study, and devotion to a higher spiritual reality. These five are meant to help regulate our inner mental life and harmonize our life with the highest spiritual goals we strive for. Purity refers to clarifying our physical, mental, and emotional selves. Contentment is a state of not wishing for more than is present in this moment. Austerity is used to help develop will-power and to create a sense of zeal for enlightenment. Self-study refers to the need for an understanding of the sacred writings of yoga and the need to study the nature of the self as well. Finally, the call for devotion is meant to increase our dedication and commitment to seek ultimate reality by casting away egotism and attachments to the individual self.

The third limb of yoga is *Postures,* or *Asanas.* These are the familiar physical postures that most people in the West associate with yoga. On a practical level, the postures are not simply to increase flexibility and relaxation. All postures are designed to enhance meditation as well. They are intended to prepare the physical body for enlightenment and samadhi, which is a dramatic mind-body experience. Again, in authentic yoga practice, the postures are only one part of an interdependent system that includes the other seven limbs of yoga.

The fourth limb is *Control of Prana,* or *Pranayama,* which is the vital energy of body and mind. As the most easily accessed element of *prana* is the breath, this limb emphasizes the control of breathing. Many of the techniques of yoga are focused on controlling the flow of prana within the body. In yoga psychology, prana, or breath, plays a major role in integrating the various sheaths of the physical-spiritual body (see chapter 3). In fact, there are ten types of prana energy, each associated with a specific vital force in the body. Collectively, these first four limbs are termed *Hatha yoga,* or the yoga of the body.

The fifth step, or limb, is *Sensory Inhibition,* or *Pratyahara.* It is concerned with the withdrawal of awareness from the five senses and from stimuli that may trap consciousness in nonspiritual distractions. This drawing attention inward is necessary to develop greater concentration.

The sixth limb is, quite logically, *Concentration,* or *Dharana.* At this step, training involves deepening focused concentration and the ability to sustain one-pointed attention.

The seventh step is *Meditation,* or *Dhyana.* At this step, the concentration that has been developed can be directed. Swami Rama says of this step, "Meditation expands the one-pointed mind to the superconscious state by piercing through its conscious and subconscious levels…all methods of yoga prepare one to reach the stage of meditation [the seventh step], for only through meditation can one reach the level of the super-conscious mind."[171] Interestingly, Swami Rama says that people who have considerable mastery with this step can exhibit parapsychological abilities such as mental telepathy or clairvoyance. In Eastern psychology, the reality of many parapsychological phenomena are accepted as a natural by-product of deep spiritual training, but are not to be sought after, because they are a distraction to practice.

The eighth and last step is *Spiritual Absorption,* or *Ultimate Samadhi.* This is the step of union with the ultimate reality, or Brahman.

BUDDHISM

The path to enlightenment in Buddhism is outlined in the Four Noble Truths. The first sermon the Buddha gave after his final enlightenment focused on these four truths. The Fourth Noble Truth is the Truth of the Noble Eightfold Path, which requires the simultaneous cultivation and alignment of eight qualities of mind and behavior. The Noble Eightfold Path offers the practical steps to solve the problem of human suffering.[172]

The First Noble Truth is that *life is suffering.* So basic was this truth to the Buddha's teaching that he said, "I teach one thing and one thing only, the truth of suffering."[173] Buddhism begins by stating what it considers the one irrefutable truth of life. Despite our wishes or attempts to change it, life always brings change—we are born, we age, we die; pain follows pleasure or joy follows heartache as surely as night follows day. Life is constant change. When we allow ourselves to acknowledge this inescapable reality, it inevitably creates anxiety, worry, fear, and insecurity.[174]

Although this statement sounds particularly morose and despondent, it is actually meant to free people from their dependence on false views of life. Rahula says, "the First Noble Truth contains, quite obviously, the ordinary meaning of suffering, but in addition it also includes deeper ideas such as imperfection, impermanence, emptiness, insubstantiality."[175] Western psychiatrist Mark Epstein proposes that a contemporary translation of the First Noble Truth might be that life is "pervasive unsatisfactoriness."[176] He further states, "The Buddha sees us all as Narcissus, gazing at and captivated by our own reflections, languishing in our attempted self-sufficiency, desperately struggling against all that would remind us of our own fleeting and relative natures."

The Second Noble Truth states that *the cause of suffering is craving or desire.* This second basic truth of Buddhism means that the cause of unhappiness is that in spite of the reality of inevitable change, we crave security, permanence, stability, and a permanent end to all doubt and difficulty. For instance, when we find something that appears to provide pleasure and stability, such as a job or a belief system, then we hold on to it for dear life. In Buddhism, this craving for something that will ensure permanent satisfaction and well-being is referred to as "attachment" or "grasping." Ultimately, this approach to life means that we suffer when we don't have what we want, and we suffer when we get what we want because we fear losing it. The Buddha said that all our attempts to control and manipulate life, so that we experience only the positive and pleasant, will eventually be doomed to failure.

The Third Noble Truth is that there is a way out of suffering. The cure is the abandonment of craving and desire as the basis for one's life. If the cause of suffering is craving, then the cure is release from that craving, which is nirvana.

The Noble Eightfold Path The Fourth Noble Truth describes the eight steps of the Noble Eightfold Path, which are the practical steps one takes to find relief from suffering. These eight steps are listed under three goals that are often referred to as the Threefold Training.[177] The first three steps relate to *morality or ethical conduct*: right speech, right action, and right livelihood. The next two steps are concerned with the development of *wisdom*: right thinking and right understanding. The last three of the eight steps are concerned with the development of *mental discipline or meditation skills*: right effort, right concentration, and right mindfulness.

In Buddhism, the basic foundations of spiritual practice are contained in the three steps of morality and ethical training: right speech, right action, and right livelihood. All Buddhists will take at least five basic precepts as guidelines for living that help them follow these three basic moral and ethical principles. The five basic precepts are as follows: not to destroy life, not to steal, not to commit adultery, not to lie, and not to drink to intoxication.

Just as there are five ethical and moral qualities to foster in Buddhism, there are also the five hindrances: lustful desires, anger, torpor or laziness, worry, and doubt. These are seen as the major obstacles to progress toward enlightenment. In addition to the five precepts, Buddhism also lists a number of both healthy and unhealthy mental factors in the perceptual and emotional domains (table 4.2 below). These mental factors also either support or undermine the practice of meditation and progress on the Noble Eightfold Path. In Hinduism, there is a similar idea about potential hindrances to spiritual development. The three *granthis*, or "knots," are seen as places associated with chakras, where spiritual energy gets blocked. Continued spiritual development requires that the practitioner "untie" the knots and release the blocked spiritual energy. In addition, Buddhism lists the Seven Factors of Enlightenment. These are both qualities to be developed by the meditator and personality traits that are present in someone who is enlightened. Practice of the Noble Eightfold Path also cultivates the Seven Factors of Enlightenment.[178] These seven factors begin with mindfulness, which is sustained and deepened by the three active factors of interest, energy, and investigation of the Dharma, as well as the three peaceful factors of tranquility, concentration, and equanimity.

Primary Mental Health Factors in Buddhism

Healthy Factors   Unhealthy Factors

Wisdom (Cognitive factors):

Healthy	Unhealthy
Insight	Delusion
Mindfulness	False View
Modesty	Shamelessness
Discretion	Recklessness
Confidence	Egoism

Compassion (Emotional factors):

Healthy	Unhealthy
Composure	Agitation
Non-attachment	Greed
Non-aversion	Aversion
Impartiality	Envy
Buoyancy	Avarice
Pliancy	Worry
Adaptability	Contraction
Proficiency	Torpor
Rectitude	Perplexity

Seven Factors of Enlightenment

Mindfulness	Tranquility
Interest or Joy	Concentration
Energy	Equanimity
Investigation & study of the Dharma	

Table 4.2: Material adapted from: Daniel Goleman (1975). Primary mental health factors in classical Buddhist psychology. Journal of Transpersonal Psychology, 7(2), pgs. 176—181. Used with permission.

A quick glance at the eightfold path of Patanjali's yoga and the Noble Eightfold Path of Buddhism shows that the two systems view training in a very similar fashion. Both begin with changes in ethical and moral behavior, follow that with more preparatory work for meditation, and end with the deeper levels of meditation practice.

TAOISM

Taoist spiritual training, like Hinduism and Buddhism, begins by emphasizing ethical behavior. In Taoism practitioners are instructed to foster the Three Jewels: compassion, moderation, and humility. Taoists believe that human beings are compassionate and caring by nature. They are innately good and must be taught to act in destructive and selfish ways. This basic assumption about human nature is similar to the ideas of some Western psychologists such as Carl R. Rogers.[179]

The necessity of humility for spiritual progress is emphasized again and again in the fundamental texts of Taoism. The *Tao Te Ching* says we should "live without possessiveness, act without presumption, and do not dwell on success,"[180] and "The sage relies on actionless activity; puts himself in the background and remains outside [the center of attention]."[181] The ideal is to become an "empty vessel" and allow the Tao to direct one's life by cultivating *wu wei*. Huston Smith has described *wu wei* as "the precious suppleness, simplicity, and freedom that flows from us, or rather through us, when our private egos and conscious efforts yield to a power not their own" [e.g., the Tao].[182] A fundamental tenet of this training is that the practitioner must stop trying to control events and allow the Tao to guide her or his life.

In Taoism it is believed that at birth we have three fundamental energies that propel existence: generative energy, spirit energy, and chi (or vital energy). Unfortunately, as we age, these dissipate, leading to ill health, old age, and death. Each type of energy can be lost through undisciplined activity in specific areas. Generative energy is lost through unregulated sexual desire, spiritual energy through unrestrained activity of the mind, and vital energy, or chi, is spent through too much emotional excitation. It is through the process of spiritual training, or inner alchemy, that the energy we have been given can be preserved or channeled.

MEDITATION

In Eastern psychologies the practice of meditation is generally considered to be absolutely essential to spiritual development. Meditative practices can be used to influence all aspects of personality, including emotions, thoughts, and behaviors. As we have seen, forms of meditation include active types, such as yoga or tai chi chuan, as well as contemplative types, such as the familiar sitting styles of meditation. Although there are a wide variety of meditation techniques, most are derived from two basic forms of sitting meditation: concentration and insight. Contemporary training in Eastern meditative disciplines typically combines the two basic styles to some degree. In fact, all forms of spiritual meditation—both Eastern and Western—seem to use one or both of these methods, regardless of the original religious or philosophical foundations.[183]

CONCENTRATION FORMS OF MEDITATION

Historically, the earliest style of meditation was concentration meditation. This style involves the cultivation of mental concentration, or one-pointedness. This form increases one-pointed concentration by restricting awareness to a single stimulus. The object that a person chooses to focus on can be almost anything. Common objects of attention for beginning meditators include one's breath; the physical sensations in one's body; specific virtues, such as compassion or loving-kindness; a specific word or *mantra*, such as Shiva, Buddha, or the sacred sound of OM; or stimuli from specific sensory modalities, such as the sight of a burning candle or the sound of bell. In fact, the specific object that is chosen to focus on defines many types of meditation.

Meditation teachers usually assign specific stimuli to serve as meditation objects based on aspects of the student's personality. For instance, the Buddha matched students with meditation objects based on four main personality types: (a) people who had tendencies toward anger and hatred; (b) those who were very excitable, lustful, or deluded; (c) people who were prone to devotion and religious faith; and (d) and those who were intellectual and less emotional.[184]

Intense concentrative meditation practice can allow a person to deepen concentration and develop progressive stages of one-pointedness. As skill develops, the person moves awareness through ever deepening levels of absorption called the *jhanas* (JAH-nas; P), until she or he experiences *samadhi*.

In Theravada Buddhism, there is a form of concentrative meditation called *samatha* (SA-ma-ta) that translates as "calm abiding" or "tranquility." Jack McGuire says, "[S]amatha meditation involves focusing one's mind on something in particular that can thereby function as a clarifying influence, keeping other thoughts and feelings at bay."[185] When this type of mediation is nurtured, it allows a person to maintain "an anomalous state of attentional balance in which a high level of attentional arousal is maintained while remaining deeply relaxed and composed."[186] Beginning meditators are often instructed to focus on their breath or "abide with" their own breathing process.

INSIGHT FORMS OF MEDITATION

The second major form of meditation is called *vipassana* (vi-PAH-sah-nah; P), insight meditation, or choiceless awareness. This form also involves focusing one's mind, but the focus of attention is more open and fluid. Vipassana meditation involves opening up attention and allowing one's awareness to quietly and dispassionately observe the creation and passing away of all elements of perception in each moment. In this type of meditation, the instructions are to expand attention to the ever-changing panorama in one's awareness without attempting to influence, alter, or compulsively react to the specific contents of the mind. The idea is to simply allow thoughts, emotions, images, and sensations to enter awareness; to fully recognize them; and then allow them to fade from awareness as they are replaced by other mental contents. This state of mind has been called "witness concentration," because a person can simply observe the creation of mental contents as a moment-to-moment experience. It is said that intense *vipassana* meditation practice can develop one's ability to observe the activity of mind to such a degree that the actual creation and dissolution of thoughts, emotions, or even one's sense of self can be calmly observed.[187] One of the many unique contributions of the Buddha was that he created the *vipassana* style of meditation.[188]

One of the first advantages of insight meditation is that it helps break the seemingly automatic links between thoughts, emotions, and impulsive behaviors. That is, it helps reduce emotional reactivity. Instead of experiencing anger and then compulsively reacting out of that anger, a person can calmly observe the presence of angry emotions in the mind and allow them to dissipate or decide on the most appropriate behavior—it helps calm the "monkey mind." Insight meditation can develop increasingly greater degrees of insight, eventually progressing through eight stages.[189] In the traditional texts, the path of insight meditation is said to lead to nirvana.

Practically, a major difference between insight meditation and the concentration form concerns potential changes to personality. In concentration forms, the attainment of even the highest *jhanas* does not permanently change personality. In contrast, each taste of nirvana permanently alters personality.

LEVELS OF CONSCIOUSNESS AND THE STAGES OF AWAKENING

The initial attempts to practice meditation often involve some degree of difficulty. As in learning any new skill, the first steps require learning new and unfamiliar behaviors. In the case of meditation, those behaviors involve controlling the activities of one's mind such as thinking, attention, and quality of awareness.[190] As a person masters the initial steps, he or she begins to move through progressive stages of spiritual development. These stages differ somewhat, depending on which type of meditation is practiced.

STAGES OF CONCENTRATION MEDITATION[191]

For most people, the first attempts to concentrate one's mental facilities on a single stimuli are met with failure, as one's mind wanders from point to point and seeks some variety to counteract boredom or to avoid facing one's inner reality. After a student has acquired some degree of skill at concentration, a moment comes when concentration becomes more intense, as the five hindrances are muted and are replaced by a sense of calm well-being. As experience with meditation develops, the practitioner moves through the next stages (see table 4.3 below).

Swami Rama has described the first steps as the four stages in the development of nonattachment. The first stage involves turning attention away from unhealthy desires and attractions. It entails making "a sincere effort to not allow the mind to dwell on sensual objects."[192] The second stage occurs when a person can calmly note the presence of desires and attachments but is no longer impelled to action or further thought. It is the stage of nonattachment where equilibrium is established. The third stage is one where the "senses have been subdued [and] the mind...can function independently of the senses."[193] The temptations of the world no longer tempt the person in the usual ways. The emotions are under some degree of control, and attention is no longer driven about by various likes and dislikes. Next is the formal starting point for the concentration path of meditation.

After the first three stages of nonattachment, the concentration path formally begins with what is called *access concentration*. At this point, the person's concentration takes a major leap toward one-pointedness, and the usual internal distractions in meditation temporarily fade away. The person may also experience bliss, happiness, equanimity, increased energy, flashes of brilliant light, or visions (although the visions may be either blissful or terrifying).

The next eight steps on the path of concentration meditation involve passage through the eight *jhanas,* or degrees of full absorption. All traditional texts describe the first four jhanas. However, differences among texts become apparent rather quickly. For instance, some view the last four as only a subset of the fourth jhana, and in Buddhist psychology the first jhana is divided into two parts.[194] The description presented here will describe the traditional eight steps on the path of concentration. The first four jhanas are referred to as the Pure Form or the Material states.[195] They are also described by referencing which of five mental factors are present in consciousness.

The Eight Jhanas, or degrees of Full Absorption The first jhana involves a break with normal waking consciousness through a total absorption in the object of meditation. At this point, all distracting thoughts and intrusive emotional desires drop away. The five mental factors present in consciousness at this point are as follows: thinking, which destroys laziness; reflecting, which destroys doubt; rapture, which destroys hatred; happiness, which destroys worry; and one-pointed concentration, which destroys greed. The first experience is very brief, but it can be sustained with further practice.

In the second jhana, any verbal thoughts about meditation stimuli drop away. Essentially, the inner verbalizations that we all use to help create a sense of reality and self-identity are no longer present. At this point, the mental factors present are rapture, happiness, and one-pointedness. Rapture is the joy we feel when we finally get something we desperately want, whereas happiness is the enjoyment of that something. Note that the two cognitive factors of thinking and reflecting have dropped away.

In the third jhana, the experience of rapture fades, leaving only happiness and one-pointedness. That is, in the third jhana, any emotional experience based on achieving important goals is dropped, leaving only the emotional experience of happiness. However, another clarification may be necessary at this point. The use of the term *happiness* may be cause for confusion, because the term can mean so many emotions to different people. In Hinduism, the emotional experience is often referred to as *bliss*, which implies a deep and profound emotional experience that has a spiritual quality at the core.

At the fourth jhana, all forms of mental and physical pleasure are transcended, while a sense of profound equanimity remains. The mental factors present are now one-pointedness and a new factor called pure equanimity. Many people might wonder why happiness and bliss are transcended—isn't the goal of meditation to find a profound sense of happiness? To answer this question, recall that even positive emotions are seen as a cause of suffering, because when we have them, we are conflicted: we are subtly afraid that the pleasant feelings will go away. The goal is to find an experience of spiritual bliss that transcends normal, dualistically based conceptions of happiness versus unhappiness.

The next four jhanas are called *Formless*, because all mental contents that define the normal way of thinking have fallen away, leaving one-pointedness and equanimity. They are often described by reference to the object of concentration that is present. At the fifth jhana, concentration turns from forms toward an awareness of the infinite space that surrounds objects of perception. The sixth jhana moves to the experience of infinite awareness or infinite consciousness. In the seventh jhana, even infinite space and consciousness fades, to be replaced by an experience of emptiness, *sunyata*, or the infinite Void. Paradoxically, the mind "takes as its object the awareness of an absence of any object."[196] At this stage, the inability of words to describe or capture the experience becomes all too obvious. Finally, the eighth jhana appears when there is no longer any sense of normal perception remaining. It is the level of consciousness before concepts and perceptions are formed. Once again, the inability of words and linguistic formulations to describe these experiences creates a sense of paradox and ineffability that is unavoidable. Table 4.3 below shows the sequential stages of consciousness experienced with the concentration form of meditation.

Stages of Concentration Meditation

1. Four Stages of Non-attachment:

> Turning attention away from unhealthy desires.
> Calmly note the presence of desires & attachments.
> Senses have been subdued.
> Access Concentration.

2. The Eight Jhanas:

> a. Jhanas of Form:
>> Total absorption in the object.
>> Verbalizations drop away.
>> Emotional experiences drop away.
>> Equanimity.
> b. Formless Jhanas:
>> Awareness of infinite space.
>> Infinite consciousness.
>> The Void, Sunyata.
>> Neither perception nor non-perception.

Table 4.3: Stages of consciousness in concentration meditation.

STAGES OF INSIGHT MEDITATION

In the traditional texts, the stages of insight meditation can only begin when the student has mastered either one of two basic meditation skills. The first skill is the ability to enter access concentration, which was described in the previous section. The second point of entry into insight meditation can be achieved by experiencing what is called *bare attention*. With this skill, the meditator can calmly observe the changing landscape of her or his thoughts and emotions without being constantly drawn away into fantasy, reactive streams of thought, or other psychological and emotional distractions. This degree of mental control is equivalent to access concentration, although the two are attained through different meditation strategies.

After the first skill level is achieved, the formal stages of insight meditation begin with the first stage called *mindfulness* (*sattipatthana* in Pali*).* The practice of mindfulness is basic to all forms of insight meditation. In fact, the practice of mindfulness is absolutely essential to most forms of spiritual training. The Buddha's discourse on the topic is contained in the *Satipatthana-sutta* (*"The Setting up of Mindfulness"*). This discourse is so highly regarded that some Buddhist monks use it as a daily chant.

Mindfulness is a practice in which a person gently stays with objects of attention as an interested observer. Essentially, mindfulness is paying attention to the moment-to-moment details of one's life. The experience of mindfulness has also been described as meta-attention, or paying attention to awareness itself.[197] Daniel Goleman's excellent description of mindfulness may be helpful at this point:

> In mindfulness, the meditator methodically faces the bare facts of his [sic] experience, seeing each event as though occurring for the first time. He does this by continuous attention to the first phase of perception, when the mind is *receptive* rather than reactive. He restricts his attention to the bare notice of his senses and thoughts. He attends to these as they arrive in any of the five sense or in his mind, which in the Visuddhimagga [i.e., a classical Buddhist text on meditation] constitutes a sixth sense. While attending to his

sense impressions, the meditator keeps reaction simply to registering whatever he observes. If further comment, judgment, or reflection arises in the meditator's mind, these are themselves made the
focus of bare attention. They are neither repudiated nor pursued but
simply [allowed to dissipate] after being noted.[198]

In traditional Buddhism, mindfulness meditation takes four basic objects
as its focus: the body, emotions or sensations, mental states or moods,
and mental concepts. That is, the focus of mindfulness can be physical
sensations (e.g., pain in one's legs), emotions (e.g., emerging joy and
contentment), thoughts (e.g., "I wonder when this meditation period
will end"), or mind objects (e.g., memories and images of childhood).
Whatever the focus, the meditator's response is identical—to observe
without reactivity. Each is observed dispassionately and viewed as
momentary experiences that arise and fade. Mindfulness corrects our
tendency to attach to sensory and psychological experiences and perceive
them as real. Initial skill at mindfulness is followed by true insight
meditation, which develops a "clear and single-minded awareness of
what actually happens to us and in us at the successive moments of
perception."[199]

With further practice, the path of insight meditation continues to
the second stage—*reflections*. At this stage, the student realizes that
the contents of the mind are distinct from the mind that contemplates
those phenomena. That is, the process of awareness is separate from the
objects of awareness. As this stage continues, the student comes to the
realization that there is no permanent self behind this process. There
is no permanent psychological entity that directs this process. Instead,
innumerable causes and conditions fuel the arising and passing away of
these psychological moments we call the self (see "Dependent origination" in chapter 3).

The third stage is called *pseudonirvana*, because the student can
believe the experiences of this stage are true nirvana. This stage begins
when the student begins to "see clearly the beginning and end of each
successive moment of awareness."[200] Along with this awareness can
come feelings of rapture and bliss, vigorous energy, feelings of intense
happiness or devotion, visions of brilliant light, along with a deep sense
of tranquility and equanimity. If the student is practicing under the

guidance of a competent teacher, these phenomena will be understood as dramatic and compelling visions that need to be transcended if progress is to be made.

The fourth stage, which is called *realization,* can be difficult for the practitioner. At this stage, each fading moment of perception is seen so clearly that the perceptual world of the student is seen as constantly dissolving. Everything is change, there is nothing permanent to grasp. There is no permanent solid ground of experience to hold on to. Even pleasurable experiences arise and fade away. For a number of people, this stage is marked by despair, a loss of hope, and fear as everything that one's life has been based on appears to be an illusion and a fantasy. In Christian mysticism, this experience is known as the "Dark Night of the Soul."[201] The release from this despair comes by continuing one's meditation practice even deeper.

Further practice brings the student to the fifth stage of *effortless insight.* The despair of the previous stage is left behind, replaced by effortless insight into the deepest nature of all arising psychological phenomena. He or she notices with precise clarity and calm detachment the exact moment when all perceptual phenomena, including any idea of a "self," first appear in awareness and then fade away.

The student is now ready for the sixth stage—the experience of true *nirvana.* At this point, all mental phenomena cease entirely, and consciousness no longer has an object. As was discussed in chapter 3, the theory of dependent origination states that all phenomena arise due to numerous causes and conditions—they are all the result of prior conditioning. Nirvana, however, is described as the "unconditioned state," or that which is beyond all conditioning. In Eastern psychology, the experience of nirvana permanently eliminates a certain portion of negative personality traits. The degree of this change depends on the depth of nirvana experienced.

After the first experience of nirvana, the meditator is known as a *stream enterer.* At this point, the person has entered the stream that will flow inevitably toward full enlightenment within no more than seven more lifetimes. Further practice results in a *once returner,* who will reach full enlightenment in either the current life or the next. Continued practice results in a *nonreturner,* who will be completely liberated in this lifetime. It is indeed a rare person who progresses even further to become an arhat. At this point, the person has totally eliminated all negative emotions, thoughts, and behaviors from her or his personality. As mentioned earlier, Western psychology has no theoretical perspective that describes, or even recognizes, this degree of mental training.

Eastern theories of mental health actually propose another stage of insight meditation in addition to nirvana. This depth of insight is only available to a nonreturner or an arhat who has also mastered all eight jhanas. It is a stage called *nirodh*, or total cessation. During nirvana, consciousness ceased to have an object. In *nirodh*, consciousness completely ceases. Note that this is not unconsciousness, but rather "supraconsciousness." Practitioners at this level can enter into profound states of concentration and absorption that may last for days, at least in normal time.

The seven stages of consciousness experienced with the insight form of meditation are summarized below:

1. Mindfulness.

2. Reflections.

3. Pseudonirvana

4. Realization

5. Effortless Insight

6. True Nirvana

7. Nirodh

STAGES OF TAOIST MEDITATION

In Taoist personality theory, the spiritual process is described using images and metaphors of both alchemy and birth. The process of transforming the energies of the body is expressed as igniting the internal "fires" to refine the energies in various tan-t'iens (or dan tiens) and "cauldrons." The "firing" and process of moving the refined energies through the body are controlled by meditation practices. The spiritual adept must create an "immortal fetus" and "give birth" to a new, spiritual self. Breathing practices are especially important to these processes. Rapid, or yang, breathing is used to direct processes in the middle and upper tan-t'iens, while slow, or yin, breathing is used later to direct the process of maturing the immortal fetus.

Spiritual training for the Taoist is divided into either two or three basic stages.[202] In those sects that emphasize training the body before the mind, there are three stages. The first stage of the three-stage system works with the skeletal system and internal organs to prepare it for the rigors of spiritual training. The body is strengthened by massage, calisthenics, tai chi chuan, and chi-kung postures (which are similar to yoga postures). Sitting and walking meditation, along with lifestyle and attitude changes, help quiet the mind to produce stillness and tranquility.

All sects of Taoism practice the next two stages of training. The next stage (first or second stage, depending on the sect) is divided into three substages. The first substage is focused on gathering generative energy, which is stored in the lower tan-t'ien. One of the major practices is the regulation of sexual activity and desire. For some sects, techniques of sexual yoga are utilized here (see "Tantra and sex" below). The next substage involves using breathing techniques to ignite the fires of the furnace in the lower tan-t'ien. This helps refine the generative energy into vital energy that rises into the middle tan-t'ien. In the third substage, the task is to refine the vital energy, or chi, which then rises to the upper tan-t'ien. In order to accomplish this, the emotions must be controlled. Different breathing practices are used to control mood swings, regulate emotionality, and help eliminate negative emotions, which are especially harmful to the goals of this substage. Once the chi has risen, it can be directed through the macro- and microcosmic orbits as well as the thrusting channel (see chapter 3).

The final stage of Taoist training begins by refining spirit energy in the upper tan-t'ien. Meditation practices at this point focus on emptying the mind of discursive thoughts, transcending the duality of subject and object, and entering a state of emptiness, or the Void, similar to what Buddhists describe. When the process is fully developed, the three energies of the body can rise to the top of the head in a process referred to as the "Three Flowers Gathering at the Top of the Head." In addition, all energy blockages in the body dissolve, and the yin and yang energies merge in a process called the "Copulation of the Dragon and the Tiger." The gathering of the refined and transmuted energies creates the "Golden Flower," the "Golden Elixer," or the "Golden Pill."

The metaphors and imagery of the next step come from pregnancy and birth. After the Golden Pill is formed, it descends into the abdomen and forms the Immortal Fetus, which must be incubated in the body. Meditative practices at this point involve further refining the energies while the practitioner resides in a place of peace, quietude, and seclusion. After "pregnancy" is completed, the "fetus" matures, rises to the top of the head, and is "born" as the energies exit the body to merge with the Tao. Further practice allows the energy of the Tao to move freely back and forth between the person and the natural world.

The instructions for practicing Taoist yoga can be incredibly involved and intricate. As an example, take a look at the following instructions for moving chi through the microcosmic orbit. Please note that I have edited (and simplified!) the instructions in this passage to make it more readable.

> First stop your thinking...Then knock the lower teeth against the upper ones 36 times to stabilize both body and spirit...Then roll your tongue in your mouth 36 times directing your (closed) eyes to follow its movement...Calm your mind and count your breath 360 times...Now swallow one third of your saliva which should follow (the vital principle) down to the Bright Palace (the heart) before returning to the ocean of prana (the lower belly)...Rest for a little, and with your hands, rub the lower belly 180 times...Then chafe the backs of the thumbs against each other until they are hot and, with them, rub the eyes 14 times to quench the "fire" in the heart, the nose 36 times to refresh the lungs, the ears 14 times to invigorate the kidneys, and the face 14 times to strengthen the spleen...Conclude by rubbing the back of the head 24 times, the small of the back 180 times and the middles of the soles 180 times.[203]

Descriptions of Taoist meditation may also include accounts of involuntary shaking and vibrating of a person's limbs or even the whole body and also a sense that the person's body is emitting, or even radiating, bright light.[204] The literature of Hinduism and Buddhism also contain references to light being emitted by advanced meditation practitioners. Eastern practitioners have sometimes suggested that the descriptions in the Bible of saints with halos around their heads are actually referring to this phenomenon.

While the highly poetic imagery of Taoism can seem obscure, it helps to recognize similarities with other systems of Eastern thought. Primarily, the process is quite similar to the kundalini yoga system. Note that both systems describe fairly similar processes by which energy travels throughout the body as a result of spiritual practices.

COMPARING STYLES OF MEDITATION

Although the concentration and the insight forms of meditation use different methods, they both share a few common goals. At the highest stages, consciousness is released from its dependence on prior conditioning, which is the root of human unhappiness. In addition, the self is seen as impermanent and illusory. Rather than being frightful, in the proper context, this experience provides immense freedom and joy.

Therefore, although practitioners of the different Eastern perspectives may describe meditation experiences in quite different ways, the basic outline of the stages on the path of meditation is very similar. Interestingly, the paths of Christian, Jewish, and Islamic mysticism show a sequence of stages and changes in consciousness that are quite similar to the paths described in Hindu and Buddhist meditation texts.[205]

THE VARIETIES OF MEDITATION TECHNIQUES

Sometimes, all the discussions on alternate states of consciousness can obscure the fact that the final goal of meditation practice is to bring a new sense of well-being into one's every waking moment. As this is the final goal, almost any daily activity can be used as a focus for meditation. Sitting meditation is the foundation of most spiritual practices, but it is not the only method used. In fact, for the enlightened master, each and every activity of daily life is an expression of the deepest spiritual truths.

WALKING MEDITATION

One of the more common activities used as a form of meditation is walking. In many monasteries in the East, some form of walking meditation is included in the daily rituals. As with other forms of meditation, the ways in which walking is used can show considerable variation. Walking can be done quickly or slowly, for long or short periods of time, and over short or long distances. In all instances, however, the basic idea is to focus one's attention on the simple act of walking. The most common use of walking meditation is to alternate periods of walking and sitting meditation.

Some practice forms will place considerable emphasis on walking; at times it may be a practitioner's sole form of meditation practice. The Vietnamese Zen master Thich Nhat Hahn (TICK not Hahn) has become quite well known for his walking meditation retreats. During these retreats, participants may walk slowly throughout the entire day, trying to be mindful of each step. He may advise students to "[w]alk as if you were kissing the earth with your feet" or to imagine that "every step makes a flower bloom under your feet."[206] Walking may also be done over substantial distances.[207] In all religious traditions, Eastern or Western, these are called *pilgrimages*. Occasionally, walking is combined with a physical difficulty, such as walking barefoot over rocky, difficult mountainous areas.[208] However, austerities such as this are neither common nor required meditation practices.

CHANTING AND MANTRA

Another activity that is generally part of daily meditative practice is chanting. Again, there is significant variety in how chanting is used. Some chants can be quite short, whereas others may take hours to complete. Some may be part of a daily ritual, and others are done only on special occasions. Curiously, chants may be in a language that is completely unknown to the practitioner, or sections of the chant may be repeated over and over again in a fairly random order. Especially in Hinduism, the belief is that the sound or the vibration of the chant is the basis for the meaning of the words.

Related to the topic of chanting is the idea of the *mantra*. A mantra is a short word or phrase that is repeated over and over. The repetition of a *mantra* can enhance and deepen meditation. The shortest and most famous mantra is the Sanskrit word *OM*. In Hinduism the sound of OM is the most sacred of all the mantras. In fact, many chants begin and end with the chant OM.

Other examples of mantras include asking people to repeat words such as "peace" or "love" or to repeat the various names of Hindu gods or Buddhist bodhisattvas. Constant repetition is believed to act as a focus for concentration in meditation, and the person may begin to incorporate the psychological qualities associated with the word. As with chanting, some mantras are in languages that are unfamiliar to the practitioner. It is the sound of the mantra that is considered to be important, not its literal meaning.

A common Buddhist mantra is called the loving-kindness or *metta* (*P*) meditation. This simple meditation asks the person repeat to themselves the following:

May I be filled with loving-kindness.

May I be well.

May I be peaceful and at ease.

May I be happy.

After a time, practitioners will begin to expand the focus of the chant to other people such as friends, family, and benefactors (i.e., "May [person's name] be filled with loving-kindness...."). When the person is ready, he or she will expand this meditation to the most difficult people in her or his life, sending them a wish to be well and happy.[209] This can be quite a test as a person tries to develop a truly universal sense of compassion for others. Some meditation retreats will be entirely devoted to repeating this lovely little chant over and over for days at a time.

In the West, chanting is also a part of many religious practices. Many Christians recite (or chant) the Lord's Prayer, and Catholics will recite the Hail Mary. The early use of Gregorian chants evolved into plainsong and eventually turned into sacred hymns. Today this legacy is found in the profoundly beautiful sacred music of the Western tradition.

BOWING

We have already seen one type of meditation focused on the body—walking meditation. Another simple meditation focus is on bowing. Most people are familiar with the Eastern greeting, in which both palms are put together in front of the chest and a short bow is given to the other person. In Hinduism, this gesture communicates to the other person, "I salute the god within you."

This simple bow can be turned into another type of meditation by expanding the half bow from the waist into a deep full prostration in which one's whole body is brought down to the floor and brought back upright again. Particularly in Buddhist traditions, practitioners may repeat this deep bow thousands of times as a type of meditation practice. One meditation practice in Tibetan Buddhism involves 100,000 deep bows being done over a set period of time. Again, the idea is to use the physical movement as a focus for meditation.

MUDRA AND VISUALIZATION

Another form of meditation that focuses on the body is the use of *mudras*. These are specific positions of the hands and fingers that are meant to enhance meditation. All statues and images of Hindu gods and goddesses as well as Buddhist images of the Buddha and various bodhisattvas have the hands positioned in various mudras. They are meant to embody the movement of energy throughout the body during meditation and the spiritual qualities that the practitioner hopes to acquire. Most instructions on sitting meditation will include a specific mudra or position of the hands.

A frequent meditation practice involves using visualization. In these practices, the person may imagine a particular image of a god or a bodhisattva. The person may try to incorporate the particular psychological aspects of that image into his or her own life. In Tibetan Buddhism, the use of visualization in meditation has achieved considerable attention, and many monks are extraordinarily skilled. Sometimes frightening images will be used in order to help practitioners control their own emotional responses (see "Tibetan Book of the Dead" below).

THE CREATIVE ARTS

Eastern culture has brought meditation into all forms of the arts. In many ways, the discipline, focus, and mindfulness required of creative artists is a highly appropriate vehicle for spiritual practice. For instance, Indian classical music is designed to help bring the listener to alternate states of awareness and to give a glimpse of the larger reality of Brahman. The most familiar example to many westerners is the sitar music of Ravi Shankar.[210] Like music, the formal study of dance in India is based on a spiritual orientation, in this case the use of movement as a spiritual practice. The same can be said of most other classical arts of India.

In Japan, the influence of Zen has permeated almost every aspect of the culture, especially the arts. Zen influence can be seen in all the usual forms of artistic expression such as painting, pottery, music, and drama, as well as in a number of uniquely Japanese artistic forms such as haiku poetry, flower arrangement, sumi-e ink brush painting, archery,[211] gardening, and the tea ceremony. In each of these art forms, the artistic activity is used as a focus of attention and a way to express a connection with the larger reality that underlies our everyday experiences.[212]

MEDITATION TECHNIQUES IN SPECIFIC TRADITIONS

Some interesting elements of spiritual practice have evolved within specific traditions. Although many of these are not necessarily exclusive to specific religious traditions, they are often associated with Hinduism, Buddhism, or Taoism.

HINDUISM

Siddhis In most eastern spiritual traditions, the attainment of paranormal abilities is assumed to be a by-product of advanced skill in meditation. In Hinduism, these skills are known as *siddhis,* or yogic powers. They can include the development of various parapsychological abilities such as clairvoyance (i.e., knowing the future), telepathy (i.e., non-verbal communication between minds), and extraordinary physical abilities.

In India, a number of yogis have demonstrated their special powers in highly unusual ways. In the 1970s, Drs. Elmer and Alice Green of the Minninger Foundation invited Swami Rama of the Himalayan Institute to the United States. During these visits, Swami Rama's physical abilities were tested with modern scientific equipment. Western medicine assumes it is impossible to voluntarily control certain aspects of the involuntary nervous system. Nonetheless, Swami Rama demonstrated the ability to voluntarily put his heart into atrial flutter, which appeared to stop his heart when measuring his pulse. Swami Rama and other meditation masters have demonstrated extraordinary levels of physiological control when they have been measured with scientific instruments.[213]

Advanced practitioners in Buddhism and Taoism have also reported paranormal experiences. Taoist literature in particular often contains stories of extraordinary abilities of sages and masters. For example, in the autobiography of Wang Liping, a twentieth-century Taoist master, he recalls a number of powers exhibited by his meditation teachers. These included the ability to heal people who were sick but lived many miles away, the ability to read other people's thoughts, and other powers that are completely impossible from the laws of physics. At one point, Master Liping talks about a teacher who could disappear before his eyes and another teacher who could project his image into Liping's consciousness and carry on conversations completely inside Liping's mind.[214] Unlike some of the extraordinary abilities studied in India, most claims of Taoist sages have never been tested with scientific tools.

Tantra Some forms of meditation are a systematized combination of a number of the techniques listed thus far. One of the better-known forms is a system called *tantra*, which is practiced as part of both Hinduism and Tibetan Buddhism (see chapter 1). In fact, much of Tibetan Buddhism is based on tantric teachings. Tantra is a practice form that combines reading certain sacred texts, sitting meditation, chanting or mantra, visualization, the use of mandalas (see below), and other practices into a single system of spiritual training. Practitioners of tantra believe that it represents an accelerated path to enlightenment. Followers believe that enlightenment is possible in this lifetime, and a person need not slowly purify themselves over many lifetimes. The specific teachings of tantra are quite esoteric and are only given to students in the context of a student-teacher relationship. Some of the techniques are considered psychologically dangerous to the uninitiated and must be supervised by a highly trained guru or tantric master.[215]

Tantra and Sex. For many people in the Western world, their only knowledge of tantric practices comes from the association of tantra and ritualized sexual activity. This association is based on techniques that work with energy in the body, such as kundalini energy and sexual energy. Rather than suppressing sexual energy, some tantric practices try to work with it for spiritual purposes.

All of the Eastern psychologies are more comfortable with sexuality than are many religious systems in the West. Eastern cultures view sexuality as a healthy expression of the life force. Anyone from a Western culture who has seen Hindu temples may be somewhat curious about the carvings that sometimes surround those temples. Often the carvings are of men and women portrayed in very sensual postures. The men are often bare-chested, active, and powerful, while the women are shown with bare breasts and undulating hips. Inside some of the temples can be found altars that symbolically depict the male and female genitalia—the lingam and the yoni, respectively.

Although Eastern psychologies recognize that sexuality can be a hindrance to spiritual practice—most monks, for instance, take vows of celibacy—the creative power of sexuality is celebrated and even worshipped as a potential source of spiritual energy. In tantra, as well as in some forms of Taoism, this source of power can be utilized in the form of highly ritualized sexual activity. Eastern iconography and statuary often use sexual union as a symbol for the uniting of opposites of life such as yin and yang. For instance, Tibetan Buddhist statuary may depict deities in a ritualized position of sexual intercourse called *yab-yum*. In these statues, the male sits in meditation with a female sitting on his lap, facing him. This image of sexual intercourse represents the union of wisdom and compassion.

Probably because sexuality is so repressed in many Western religions, many people in the West are fascinated by tantric sexual practices.

However, only the "left-hand school" of tantra practices the actual use of ritualized sexual activity. Even in this school, many gurus see sexual activity as too easily perverted by inexperienced practitioners. In the "right-hand school," the union of male and female energies is visualized as a way to transform this polarity into spiritual union. As disappointing as it may be to curious libertines, it should be mentioned that in authentic tantric practices, the goal is not to achieve orgasm. Rather, the practice involves using the energy of sustained arousal to generate kundalini energy. In fact, the physiological and emotional release associated with orgasm is actually counterproductive to the production of kundalini.[216]

Certain Taoist sects also use sexuality as a spiritual practice. Those who practice the "paired path" use sexual arousal to help with alchemical transformations.[217] Also in this practice, the generative energy created during arousal is turned back into the body before it is dissipated through orgasm.

TIBETAN BUDDHISM

Mandalas In Tibetan Buddhism, monks have created a number of unique styles of meditation. Mandalas are visual representations of Buddhist teachings that are often filled with multiple Buddhist images and iconography (see the "Wheel of Life" in chapter 3). The creation of these mandalas can be used as a way to focus concentration while also focusing on spiritual themes and ideals. Many people in the West have seen monks create large mandalas out of colored sand. A small group of monks may work for weeks to create a beautiful, intricate mandala by scraping sand-like particles to form the design. When it is complete, they scoop it all up and throw the sand into a river as a way to express nonattachment.

Tummo (or gTum-mo) One tantric technique associated with Tibetan Buddhism results in raising the meditator's body temperature and metabolism. The meditation is called *tummo* and has been the subject of research studies in the West. In one study done at Harvard University, cold sheets were placed over the shoulders of advanced Tibetan Buddhist monks during meditation. The monks showed an ability to raise their body temperature, so that the sheets actually began to emit steam. The sheets were completely dry in about one hour.[218]

The Tibetan Book of the Dead Some of the most unusual meditation practices in Eastern psychology are associated with Tibetan Buddhist beliefs about death and rebirth. According to this tradition, there are forty-nine days between a person's death and their rebirth in another life. A book titled the *Bardo Thodol*, which is known in the West as *The Tibetan Book of the Dead*, describes the states of consciousness (the *bardos*) that are experienced on this forty-nine-day journey.[219] This text was purportedly written by the eighth-century CE tantric master Padmasambhava, who was one of the founders of Tibetan Buddhism. In addition to describing the after-death experience, the book is also a manual that prescribes certain rituals, chants, incantations, and specialized meditations to be done by the living that will help the departed person's spirit either leave the cycle of rebirths or be reborn in a better next life. One of the most fascinating aspects of the book is that the descriptions of the after-death experiences are quite similar to near-death experiences reported by people in the West today.[220]

Certain meditation practices have developed around the ideas expressed in the *Tibetan Book of the Dead*. For instance, monks may deliberately try to induce the near-death experiences described in the book in order to familiarize themselves with both the blissful and the terrifying states of consciousness (*bardos*) prior to their own actual physical death. Other tantric practices also attempt to strengthen the practitioner's ability to confront and transcend their conditioned responses to stimuli. For instance, practitioners may be asked to meditate in unusual places such as graveyards to focus on the temporality of life and to decondition their own fears.

ZEN BUDDHISM

Koan Practice In the Zen Buddhist tradition, practitioners of the Rinzai (Japan) or Chogye (Korea) schools will use koans as part of their meditation practice. Koans are puzzles or riddles that either cannot be answered by traditional logic or require an immediate behavioral response without discursive thinking. Probably the most famous koan is, "When clapping both hands, a sound is heard. What is the sound of one hand clapping?" The idea of this koan is to present the student with a puzzle that must be answered by showing an intuitive understanding that is beyond the categories and conceptualizations of language.

For instance, with the one-hand koan, our rational minds tell us that there can be no sound from only one hand. Attempts to rationally solve this problem will all fail miserably. Instead, the student must realize that the koan is asking about the reality (i.e., the "sound") that exists before we divide up ultimate reality into discrete dichotomies of yes and no, good and bad, up and down, body and mind (i.e., before the two "hands" come together and form the rational world).

The following quote gives a very personal account of working with a koan in a Zen monastery. In this case, the koan was "What is Mu?" (i.e., What is the nature of Ultimate Reality?). This quote was written by an American artist and is listed in Philip Kapleau's book, *The Three Pillars of Zen*:[221]

> I began to sit with Mu…The first day Mu felt like a heavy lump of lead in my belly. "Melt that lead!" the Roshi commanded, but it would not melt. However, the next day I hammered with Mu and came to know that its center was a brilliant, crystalline light, like a star or diamond, so brilliant that it outlined and illuminated physical objects, dazzled my eyes, filled me with light. My body felt weightless. I thought: "This is Mu!" But the Roshi counseled, "Hallucinations! Ignore them. Concentrate harder!"
>
> By the end of that day there was no light, just drowsiness, infinite weariness…The third day my eyes would not stay open…When I fought this off, my mind was immediately filled with problems of my family and marriage…"Go deeper," the Roshi said. "Question, 'What is Mu'? to the very bottom." Deeper and deeper I went.
>
> Suddenly, my hold was torn loose and I was spinning. To the center of the earth! To the center of the cosmos! To the Center, I was There. Suddenly I knew…The Roshi said: "Now you understand that seeing Mu is seeing God." I understood.

While reports of kensho or satori experiences such as this one are very dramatic, it should be remembered that a single experience is not the goal of spiritual practices. The spiritual experiences give insight into a deeper spiritual reality and are, therefore, part of a wider perspective on spiritual training and the spiritual life.

Although koans are one of the most esoteric and baffling meditation techniques, they share some qualities with creative insights. It is fairly common for a creative breakthrough to occur after all rational attempts have failed to solve the problem. In fact, a number of researchers have commented on the similarities between koans and creative breakthroughs.[222]

Shikan-taza   Primarily in the Soto school of Zen, a form of insight meditation is advocated that is called *shikan-taza,* or "nothing but just sitting." Dogen Zenji (1200–1253 CE), the founder of the Soto school, developed this style, and he believed it was the purest form of *zazen,* or meditation. It is an intense type of choiceless awareness. In shikan-taza, the meditator is simply aware, without using any of the usual techniques to focus attention. The person doesn't count breaths, label sensations, or repeat a mantra, but is simply aware of the moment. However, even saying a person "is aware of" implies a separation of awareness and an object, so maybe it is best to say that shikan-taza is *being* the moment.

TAOISM

Qigong (or Chi Kung)[223]   People in the West who have heard about qigong will usually associate it with a series of exercises designed to foster physical health. While this is one facet of qigong, the system is quite a bit more extensive than this understanding. Dr. Yang, Jwing-Ming explains that there are actually four major approaches to qigong, each practiced for different purposes. Scholars practice qigong mainly to maintain health, prevent disease, and increase longevity by regulating the mind, the body, and the breath. Medical doctors tend to focus on healing illness that is already present. This approach often emphasizes massage, acupressure, herbal treatments, and acupuncture, as well as physical movement and exercises. Martial qigong is used as a martial art and focuses on disciplines such as tai chi chuan and kung fu. Finally, religious qigong is associated with Taoist and Buddhist monks, who use certain practices in their search for enlightenment. The elaborate practices for raising chi through the tan-t'iens that were described earlier would be part of religious qigong. Therefore, qigong refers to any formalized training or discipline that promotes one's ability to regulate qi (chi) for a number of different purposes.[224]

A complete understanding of qigong requires a familiarity with the traditional Chinese understanding of human beings, nature, the cosmos, and the intricate relationships among them. In addition to knowledge of the tan-t'iens in Taoist yoga, one must also have an understanding of the acupuncture meridians and a number of other theoretical perspectives on the relationships between humans and the natural world. Breathing practices are very important in qigong, and a number of unique practices have been developed.

For example, reverse abdominal breathing involves drawing in your abdomen when inhaling and letting it out when exhaling. Obviously, this is the reverse of how natural breathing works. Other techniques include holding one's breath and moving the chi to various organs of the body and what is called skin breathing, which involves opening and closing the pores of one's skin along with inhalation and exhalation. Qigong theory holds that there is an opening in the palms and soles of the feet through which body chi communicates with the chi outside the body. Specific breathing techniques facilitate this process. Finally, hibernation breathing is used in very advanced practitioners of religious qigong to slow down body functions to almost imperceptible levels. In theory, this type of breathing is used when a sage allows his or her spirit to leave the body and travel to other places in the world. Once again, we see a reference to extraordinary paranormal powers.

Martial Arts In China, the concentration, focus, and attention of meditation was combined with forms of military training to create the martial arts. Later, these martial arts spread to Japan and Korea. Anyone familiar with any of the Eastern martial arts such as karate, tai kwon do, or tai chi chuan will know that training involves practice in one-pointed concentration, clearing the mind of distractions, and the ability to instantly react without unnecessary internal deliberation.[225] Many martial arts masters are fond of saying that the real opponent is inside yourself—it is your own doubts, fears, and internal distracting chatter. Many martial arts masters also view certain aspects of training as ways to help direct a person's chi, which facilitates the punches and throws involved in self-defense.

CAN WE FIND THE ONE "BEST" APPROACH TO MEDITATION?

By this point in the book, a considerable number of meditation styles and techniques have been discussed. There are forms that work with concentration, insight, mindfulness, and various degrees of altered states of consciousness. A wide range of techniques have also been discussed, such as sitting meditation, yoga postures, walking, chanting, bowing, and even sex. It would be reasonable to ask if there is one form of meditation or one technique that seems to be the best one; is there one approach that clearly is the most effective in fostering well-being and a lasting sense of peace? Luckily, the answer to this question is no. All of these approaches and techniques, as well as many more, can be used effectively.

Jack Kornfield has said that the common question, "What is enlightenment?" should actually be, "What are the enlightenments?"[226] Kornfield says that the singular term *enlightenment* should be used in the plural form, because there are many different forms of enlightenment. He gives examples of enlightened meditation masters, who use various skillful means to bring the reality of enlightenment into their lives and to teach it to others. These include a focus on mindfully appreciating the moment; looking deeply into the reality of the self; and focusing on love, compassion, emptiness, wisdom, or joyful abundance. It is not the technique that is important, but rather it is the persistence, commitment, and the sincerity of one's dedication.

CLOSING THOUGHTS

This chapter has covered a wide variety of meditation practices that have evolved over the long history of Eastern psychology. I hope the discussion has also conveyed a sense that these practices are very systematic and comprehensive approaches to psychological development. It should also be apparent that the practices themselves, such as meditation and chanting, are developed in relation to both a perspective on why ultimate happiness may elude us and a set of techniques based on that perspective. That is, the practices have evolved in reference to both a definition of the problem we all face in life and a definition of the solution to that problem. The practices are the concrete steps we can take to move from the problem to the solution.

The relationships among the problem, the solution, and the means to achieve the solution are important to remember, especially for those living in the Western world. In the West, it is common to see the practices and techniques removed from their original context and used for other purposes than originally intended. Although taking the spiritual practices out of their original context may be quite helpful for certain situations, it should be done with some degree of caution. For example, a few profound insights obtained while meditating does not make a person a Zen master. Similarly, attempts to produce happiness by adding a bit of mindfulness to one's day or chanting a loving-kindness meditation may be quite helpful, but the intent and the results cannot be compared to those obtained from a disciplined, formal meditation practice.

CHAPTER 5

East Meets West

Subject and object are only one. The barrier between them cannot be said to have broken down as a result of recent experience in the physical sciences, for this barrier does not exist.

ERWIN SCHROEDINGER, WINNER OF
1933 NOBEL PRIZE FOR PHYSICS.[227]

This book opened with a quotation from Kipling, in which he questioned whether the cultures of the East and the West could ever understand each other. Today, a greater understanding has taken the first steps, while the adoption of certain spiritual practices such as meditation and yoga is well underway. However, Kipling's question obscures the fact that since the nineteenth century, a number of Western philosophers and psychologists have had an interest in areas that were related to ideas and practices from Hinduism, Buddhism, and Taoism. This chapter will begin by covering a few of the ways that ideas similar to those expressed in Eastern psychology can be found in Western philosophy and psychology. Finally, the chapter will conclude with a few comments about the influence of Eastern psychology on contemporary Western psychology, including a short review of some research studies on meditation.

A SHORT HISTORY OF "EASTERN" PERSPECTIVES IN WESTERN PSYCHOLOGY

As has been mentioned throughout this book, Eastern psychology is grounded in a contemplative approach or mysticism. In fact, mysticism has been a part of the Western world for millennia. During the Golden Age of Greece, a strong mystical element was often found in the philosophy of Plato and others. Richard Tarnas believes the recognition of a transcendent realm that can be accessed through contemplation has been a continuous influence on Western thought up to the present day. Interestingly, he also argues that this approach to knowledge has been a major influence on science. Tarnas says that the desire to understand the hidden reality that underlies the world is a major motivation in *both* science *and* mysticism.[228] During the Middle Ages, a mystical search for the nature of God was institutionalized in the monasteries of Europe and has continued to influence Western culture throughout its history.[229]

Beginning around the early part of the nineteenth century, the romantic philosophers began to emphasize human emotions, instincts, intuition, insight, and creativity. Although the philosophies of this time varied considerably, a few had ideas similar to Eastern philosophy. In particular, Arthur Schopenhauer (1788–1860) based much of his philosophy on the Four Noble Truths of Buddhism. Georg W. F. Hegel (1770–1831) believed the universe must be understood as an interrelated and dynamic unity. Hegel called this dynamic unity "The Absolute." As in Eastern psychology, he said that no statement can be made about a portion of the universe without directing attention to another aspect of reality. Henri-Louis Bergson's (1859–1941) philosophy was based on his idea of the "élan vital," vital spirit, or life force that propelled organic evolution.[230] This life force seems to be quite similar to descriptions of the Tao.

In the United States, Emerson, Thoreau, Whitman, and others helped create a new blend of religion, spirituality, and mysticism called *transcendentalism*. Transcendentalism's basic premise is that "man is the spiritual center of the universe and that in man alone can we find the clue to…the cosmos itself."[231] The second premise of the movement was that virtue and happiness were grounded in self-realization, which was partially dependent upon "the expansive or self-transcending impulse of the self, its desire to embrace the whole world in the experience of a single moment and to know and become one with that world."[232]

EARLY TENTIETH-CENTURY PSYCHOLOGY

One of the founding fathers of psychology, William James (1842–1910), was interested in Eastern psychology. He also believed psychologists should study alternate states of consciousness. In a very famous passage written early in the twentieth century, James said:

> One conclusion was forced upon my mind at that time, and my impression of its truth has ever since remained unshaken. It is that our normal waking consciousness, rational consciousness as we call it, is but one special type of consciousness, whilst all about it, parted from it by the filmiest of screens, there lie potential forms of consciousness entirely different. We may go through life without suspecting their existence; but apply the requisite stimulus, and at a touch they are there in all their completeness…No account of the universe in its totality can be final which leaves these other forms of consciousness quite disregarded.[233]

Partially due to the influence of James, some American psychologists created a specialty area called the *psychology of religion*. From the 1890s to the present, researchers in the psychology of religion have studied both Western and Eastern mysticism.

Although Sigmund Freud (1856–1939) had little to say that resembled an Eastern approach to psychology, two of his closest early colleagues, Adler and Jung, did present ideas that at least resembled certain elements of Eastern thought. Alfred Adler (1870–1937) believed that people possessed an innate drive toward "social interest" or "social feeling." This drive pushed people toward altruistic, prosocial behavior toward others. For Adler, the benchmark of mental health was the development of people's innate capacity for compassion and self-knowledge. Similarly, the two benchmarks of mental health in Buddhism are compassion and wisdom.

Early in the twentieth century, Carl G. Jung (1875–1961) developed the first complete personality theory in Western psychology that took seriously the ideas of Eastern psychology. The introductions that he wrote for translations of *The Tibetan Book of the Dead*, *The Secret of the Golden Flower*, and the *I Ching* were the some of the first serious attempts by a Western psychologist to understand Eastern thought.[234] The personality theory that Jung developed was at that time—and continues to be—one of the most unique perspectives in Western psychology. Jung believed there was a deeper unconscious, called the *collective unconscious*, which contained psychological tendencies for emotional responses and expression that were shared by all members of the human species; these tendencies are more universal and shared across cultures and even historical time periods. The contents of the collective unconscious he called *archetypes*, which could be expressed in similar ways in all cultures throughout history. For example, Photo 5.1 shows a representation of the tenth-century Gallen Priory Cross, which is located at an abandoned medieval Christian monastery in County Offaly, Ireland. The symbols on this Celtic cross—the four directions, the circle, the intertwined serpents—are all archetypal symbols that have been found in many cultures around the world throughout history.

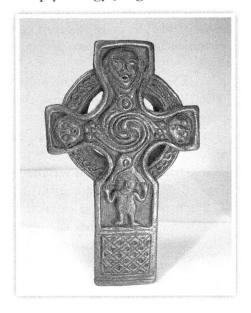

Photo 5.1: representation of the Gallen Priory Cross.

Jung believed there were many different archetypes, but the process of individuation, or optimal personality development, led to the development of the Self archetype. This is the archetype of inherent wholeness for the personality. The Self archetype could only be developed by decreasing a focus on the self-reflective ego. The de-emphasis on the control functions of the ego and a willingness to allow unconscious forces some control and direction in the personality had, for Jung, a distinctly spiritual or religious element to it. Jung certainly saw parallels between his theory and the ideas of Eastern psychology, which de-emphasizes the ego as the center of personality. In fact, Jung's ideas on the collective unconscious and personality types were heavily influenced by similar ideas from Hinduism and Buddhism.

In the early days of the twentieth century, Roberto Assagioli (1888–1974) also developed a personality theory that owed a great deal to ideas from Eastern psychology. Assagioli developed a theory of personality that he called psychosynthesis. In Assagioli's system, the psyche is roughly divided into three parts: the unconscious, the conscious, and the transpersonal unconscious.[235] He divided the transpersonal unconsciousness into two components: the transpersonal self, which was similar to Jung's descriptions of the Self archetype, and the collective unconscious, which for him was a higher consciousness associated with transcendent spiritual experiences. Assagioli believed that the spiritual dimension of life was not completely synonymous with the collective unconscious. In this respect, Assagioli was closer to the perspectives of Eastern psychology than was Jung.

Early psychodynamic thinkers who were influenced by Buddhism included Karen Horney (1885–1952) and Erich Fromm (1900–1980). Karen Horney was one of the first women to gain recognition in the psychoanalytic movement. For Horney, the experience of "basic anxiety" is a fundamental condition of being a human being. Later in her life, she adopted the Zen concept of "wholeheartedness" and said her concept of basic anxiety was similar to the first Noble Truth of Buddhism—life is suffering.[236] Erich Fromm coauthored the book *Zen Buddhism and Psychoanalysis* in 1960, which was one of the first serious comparisons between Eastern and Western theories of mental health written by experts from both perspectives.[237] Later, he offered suggestions on how to achieve his idea of optimal well-being. Fromm's practical suggestions sounded remarkably similar to Buddhist meditation practices.[238]

HUMANISTIC AND EXISTENTIAL PSYCHOLOGY

In the early 1950s, a few American psychologists created a new approach to psychology that would focus on uniquely human concerns such as meaning, creativity, and personal growth. Soon this approach would be called *humanistic psychology*. Humanistic psychology tends to emphasize the individual experiences of being human, rather than the detached objectivity and analytical methods of traditional science. Unlike most academic psychologists, many humanistic psychologists are more comfortable with research based on phenomenological methods. A phenomenological investigation attempts to study human experience as it naturally occurs in consciousness. Meditation can be considered a highly specialized type of phenomenological investigation. From its inception, humanistic psychology was heavily influenced by ideas from Eastern psychology, such as the writings of Zen scholar D. T. Suzuki. In fact, humanistic psychologists were the first to study meditation, yoga, and other techniques of personal growth from the East.

Carl R. Rogers (1902–1987) developed the concept of the fully functioning person to describe his ideas on optimal well-being. For Rogers, the fully functioning person showed three characteristics: greater openness to experience, existential living, and more trust in one's organism. Openness could be seen when a person decreased the use of defense mechanisms and allowed all experiences of life, both positive and negative, to be present in awareness. Existential living involved living fully in the moment and becoming more a participant in one's ongoing experience, rather than always trying to be in control of it. Greater trust in one's organismic experience involves being more open to one's emotions, intuitions, and preverbal reactions to life. Some psychologists have commented on the similarities between Rogers's ideas and those of Taoism.[239]

The theory of self-actualization created by Abraham Maslow (1908–1970) is the best-known perspective on optimal well-being in Western psychology.[240] His theory presents a contemporary version of Aristotle's ideas on eudaimonia, or flourishing. For both Aristotle and Maslow, optimal well-being is tied to the cultivation of higher virtues or values. For Maslow, many of these were the B-needs, or Being needs, which included ideals such as justice, truth, beauty, goodness, and aliveness.[241] Interestingly, many of the B-values and personality traits that Maslow listed are also on the list of healthy personality traits found in the Eastern psychologies, and they should be found in advanced practitioners of Eastern meditative disciplines.[242] In fact, in research studies on meditation, one of the most frequent relationships studied is between self-actualization and experience with meditation.

One section of Maslow's original self-actualization theory was a discussion of peak experiences. He saw peak experiences as those brief moments when people experienced extreme joy, wonder, or awe.[243] Maslow said these experiences could lead to greater psychological health, at least temporarily:

> [T]he main finding relevant to our topic was that an essential aspect of peak experience is integration within the person and therefore between person and the world. In these states of being, the person becomes unified; for the time being, the splits, polarities, and dissociation within him tend to be resolved; the civil war within is neither won nor lost but transcended.[244]

In very profound peak experiences, people can experience a feeling of oneness or merging with the world. In Maslow's book *Religion, Values, and Peak Experiences,* he speculates that when the reality one feels merged with is conceptualized as God, unitive peak experiences are often referred to as mystical experiences.[245] Dacher Keltner has recently studied the experience of *awe,* or "deep appreciative wonder," which is very similar to Maslow's descriptions of some peak experiences.[246]

Toward the end of his life, Maslow mentioned that peak experiences could become almost permanent ways of experiencing the world. This phenomenon he termed the *plateau experience.* During a plateau experience, all aspects of the world take on a sacred quality and are seen as manifestations of a divine reality.[247] Maslow referred to this as *resacralization,* or restoring a sense of the sacred to the ordinary world. Maslow saw this type of perception as an antidote to a new defense mechanism he named *desacralization.* This defense mechanism was operating when people repressed a sense of the sacred and saw the world as simply objects with no inherent meaning or value.

Rollo May (1909–1994) is considered the person most responsible for introducing existential philosophy to American psychology.[248] Existentialism has long been compared to Eastern psychology due to a number of similarities between the two perspectives. For instance, both assume that normal adjustment to the everyday world is based on illusions that serve to protect a limited self-ideal. Both also assume that life has the greatest and most significant sense of meaning when certain fundamental realities are addressed honestly. Those realities include our inability to escape from fundamental anxiety and the inevitability of death. Viktor Frankl (1905–1997) was another influential existential psychologist who convincingly argued that people must create their own sense of meaning from whatever circumstances life handed them.[249] Frankl said that people must be able to transcend their limited sense of self-identity and embrace values that were higher and more spiritual. He believed that acts of *self-transcendence* were a necessary hallmark of optimal mental health. Note, however, that although both Eastern psychological perspectives and existentialism posit a basic fundamental anxiety, Eastern perspectives also say there is a way to transcend the anxiety and find lasting peace of mind.

FLOW AND OPTIMAL EXPERIENCING

Mihalyi Csikszentmihalyi (b. 1934) introduced a state of consciousness into Western psychological research that he terms *flow*.[250] Flow occurs when we become totally absorbed in an activity. To use a phrase taken from Eastern psychology, during flow we become "one" with our activity, and our actions seem to happen spontaneously and without self-conscious effort. At these times, we are engaged in what he calls optimal experiencing. During intense and dramatic flow, there can be profound alterations in the perception of time, of self-identity, and the self-other boundary. In fact, when people experience flow very intensely, the phenomenological experience is clearly a type of altered state of consciousness. Csikszentmihalyi has said that when people can bring the quality of flow experiences to their daily activities, they are experiencing what he calls *engagement*. On a personal note, I remember speaking with a Zen meditation master who had read Csikzentmihalyi's original book on flow. He said that the description of flow was "pretty close" to some his experiences as a result of meditation—but certainly not all of them.[251]

TRANSPERSONAL PSYCHOLOGY

Later in his life, Maslow added a sixth need to his needs hierarchy.[252] This need was seen as higher than, or above, self-actualization. Maslow called it the need for self-transcendence. By 1968, Maslow, Frankl, Stanislav Grof, and James Fadiman had agreed upon the name "transpersonal psychology" for a new discipline that would study a spiritual psychology of transcendence.[253] Transpersonal psychology would study how transcendent experiences can be used to foster a greater sense of well-being. From its inception up to the present, transpersonal psychology has drawn heavily from theories and practices found in the East as it attempts to integrate both Western and Eastern perspectives on human psychology. Early examples of transpersonal psychologists include Carl Jung and Roberto Assagioli (discussed above). Since its formal inception in the 1970s, transpersonal-oriented psychologists have continued to investigate the spiritual dimension of life and seek ways to integrate Eastern and Western ideas about psychology. Two of these theorists deserve special mention.

Stanislav Grof and realms of the human unconscious In the early 1960s, Stanislav Grof (b. 1931) was one of the few researchers in the United States investigating the effects of psychedelic drugs on patients. The unusual, and extremely fascinating, experiences that his patients reported to him forced Grof to develop his own theory of the unconscious.[254] In Grof's theory, the psychedelic experience can invoke four levels of the unconscious.

Grof's theory begins with what he calls the *aesthetic level*, which is the most superficial level and represents visual images, auditory hallucinations, and sensory stimulations. Many casual users of psychedelics never move beyond this level. At the second level, the *psychodynamic level*, Grof's patients seemed to access repressed unconscious material that supported some of Freud's ideas on personality. The next level of the unconscious Grof calls the *perinatal level*. The basic experiences at this level tended to be very difficult and emotionally demanding. Often they could be a catalyst for an existential crisis in which the person faced emotional issues of death and psychological rebirth. Interestingly, Grof states that everyone who confronted the experiences at this level and resolved them discovered the utmost relevance of the spiritual or religious dimension to human experience.

The last level of the unconscious Grof calls the *transpersonal level*. This level is a rather complex amalgam of a number of experiences. For example, Grof's patients reported experiences that appeared to support Jung's theory of a collective unconscious, as well as experiences that bore a striking resemblance to phenomena described in Kundalini yoga. Finally, some patients also reported mystical experiences that were thoroughly consistent with descriptions from Christian and Eastern mysticism.

Ken Wilber and the spectrum of consciousness Unquestionably, the most comprehensive transpersonal theory of personality is the perspective of Ken Wilber (b. 1949). In a series of groundbreaking books, he created a theory that postulated sequential stages to personality development, which encompassed both Western and Eastern ideas about personality.[255] In his later works, he presents a theory that combines individual personality development, social organization, and the historical development of cultural worldviews.

Wilber views psychological growth as a developmental stage process that goes beyond the stages associated with personal growth in Western psychology. In Wilber's model, each stage involves a number of transformations in the emotional, cognitive, and interpersonal components of the sense of self. Each stage involves a separation-individuation struggle, as the old sense of identity and self confronts an emerging new perspective that demands reorientation and readjustment to an expanded perspective on self and reality.   Wilber's model of development involves ten stages, although Wilber says that the last one is not actually a stage. The first six stages have been described quite well by a number of Western psychologists, such as Erik Erikson and Jane Loevinger, and will not be discussed here. Stages 7 through 10 describe transpersonal development.

At stage 7, a person begins to transcend his or her self-concerns and feels an empathic identification with all humanity. Western psychologists such as Maslow have occasionally described this stage. Stage 8 involves access to Jungian archetypes, the deeper stages of meditation, and transcendental insights and rapture. At stage 9, the sense of an individual self falls away, to be replaced by an experience of oneness and unity with all of existence. The last "stage" is the experience of complete oneness with God, Brahman, Buddha nature, the Tao, or whatever is seen as the Ultimate Reality. It is interesting to note the parallels between Wilber's stages and the chakra system. Wilber's ideas have been criticized as too broad and extremely difficult to test with empirical research methods. Nonetheless, he has helped open the door for the study of how Western and Eastern psychologies have approached the topic of mental health and well-being.

EAST-WEST PSYCHOLOGY IN THE TWENTY-FIRST CENTURY

In contemporary Western psychology, some of the resistance to ideas from Eastern psychology has faded. In fact, at the beginning of the twenty-first century, it was clear that influences from an Eastern perspective on psychology were beginning to have an impact on Western psychology. Articles began appearing in professional journals that presented ideas from Eastern psychology as alternative scientific hypotheses about human psychological systems. For example, a 2006 article in the *American Psychologist* presented Buddhist ideas on mental health and well-being.[256] A 2005 article in *Current Directions in Psychological Science* by Paul Ekman and others presented Buddhist ideas on emotions.[257] Dramatic brain imaging studies of Richard Davidson and others (see below) generated quite a bit of interest from scientists around the world. Davidson and Ekman have also participated in a series of seminars with the Dalai Lama on how Western scientific tools can be used to help understand the parameters of optimal well-being.[258] Finally, mysticism remains an active area of research in the psychology of religion.[259]

RESEARCH ON MEDITATION

The most influential reason ideas from Eastern psychology are now of interest to some Western psychologists is because of positive results from studies of meditation. In particular, over the years numerous research studies have found that meditation can help reduce a number of problems including anxiety, hypertension, drug addiction, and chronic pain.[260] While the results of these studies offer needed hope to people who suffer from these problems, the classic literature on meditation does not mention these problems as the fundamental reason for meditative practices in a spiritual context. However, a number of studies have investigated hypotheses more relevant to the literature from Eastern psychology. Some of these have looked at how meditation affects perception, emotions, biological processes, and well-being. Research on the concentration form of meditation has been represented mainly by investigations of Indian yogis and, most impressively, by the Transcendental Meditation organization.[261] There are over six hundred studies that have looked at the impact of transcendental meditation on behavior. Research on the insight form has focused mostly on Buddhist meditation styles.[262] It should be noted, however, that a much smaller number of studies have investigated meditation by using practitioners who have many years of experience with meditation. Of course, an adequate test of most claims made by the Eastern psychologies requires the use of advanced practitioners of meditation. The brief review below will primarily cover studies that have used meditators with significant experience with meditation.

Psychological Studies Most of the classical meditation texts say that meditation should produce a sense of calmness, composure, equanimity, and detachment from emotional turmoil. In fact, studies of experienced meditators have found that meditation can induce experiences such as equanimity, tranquility, bliss, detached neutrality, and a sense of selflessness.[263] Subjects also report experiences that are ineffable (difficult to describe in words), as well as feelings of bliss, rapture, sublime happiness, and the buildup and release of energy during meditation sessions. Some of these experiences clearly seem analogous to the release of kundalini energy. Similarly, Westerners report altered self-concepts such that normal subject-object boundaries dissolve, leaving a feeling of oneness and altered perceptions of time and space. Examples of what appears to be extrasensory perception have also been reported.

For example, a study by Karlis Osis, Edwin Bokert, and Mary Lou Carlson, along with a replication and extension by Richard Kohr, asked general questions about the phenomenological experiences that occur during meditation.[264] Both studies found that meditation changed consciousness in rather consistent ways. People reported that they felt a sense of merging or oneness with others, a sense of presence, a transcendence of space and time, serenity, love and joy, and, in some cases, flashes of brilliant light. They also described experiences that occasionally made meditation uncomfortable or difficult. Kohr summarized the studies thus: "Both sets of data suggest a distinct change in the way of experiencing. Often there seems to be a sense of having transcended the limitations of three-dimensional reality; a melting of the psychological barriers between oneself and others. A sense of the sacred frequently occurred in this highly valued state of awareness."[265]

One of the more interesting studies of experienced meditators involved a study of experienced Buddhist meditators.[266] Daniel Brown and Jack Engler studied classic Buddhist meditation texts in order to create an objective scale by which to measure meditation experiences. They also used meditators from an intensive three-month meditation retreat, other advanced students of meditation, and a few Asian meditation masters who had experienced enlightenment. Brown and Engler found evidence that the intensive practice of meditation can produce changes in cognition and perception that are entirely consistent with the traditional literature on Buddhist meditation.

Recent work on the advantages of positive emotion has sparked a few studies on a type of Buddhist meditation called loving-kindness (or "metta") meditation (see chapter 4). This meditation is designed to help generate positive emotions such as compassion, love, generosity, and tolerance. Studies using this style of meditation have shown dramatic changes in brain functioning (see "Physiological Studies" below). In addition, even novice meditators can gain substantial benefits from this type of meditation.[267]

Research on yoga and tai chi chuan has also shown the benefits of these styles of active meditation. Although studies are not as extensive as those on sitting meditation, they are nonetheless supportive of the benefits.[268]

Mindfulness Meditation *Mindfulness* has emerged in recent years as one of the more useful concepts to come out of Eastern psychology. Mindfulness meditation is a style in which people pay attention to the ongoing experience of their life without interference, reactivity, or avoidance. Jon Kabat-Zinn introduced ideas from Buddhist mindfulness meditation into Western psychology through studies designed to help people manage chronic pain. The system he created is called *mindfulness-based stress reduction* (MBSR) and combines elements of mindfulness meditation, yoga, and group support. In later studies, he found that MBSR was useful in dealing with anxiety and other problems. Numerous studies by other researchers followed and sparked significant interest in mindfulness meditation techniques. Today, mindfulness meditation has been found useful in a wide variety of areas, including the treatment of anxiety, depression, and substance abuse.[269] Studies have also found that the practice of mindfulness meditation can help therapists be more focused and aware for their clients. Interestingly, one study found that psychotherapy clients were more satisfied with therapists who practiced Zen meditation, even when the clients were unaware of this fact.[270]

Physiological Studies Physiological studies of Indian yogis and Zen Buddhist monks were among the first scientific studies of meditation.[271] Researchers have found that many profound spiritual experiences do produce consistent physiological effects that can be measured with contemporary techniques of science.

Studies that looked at the brain waves of people while meditating have been very common. Although measuring brain waves can only give a rough indication of brain activity, the results have been intriguing. For instance, Herbert Benson and his colleagues studied the metabolism and EEG patterns in three highly experienced Tibetan monks.[272] They found that the monks could significantly alter their body metabolism rates during meditation. The EEG readings during meditation also showed significant alterations with increased beta activity (fast waves found during focused activities). Interestingly, other studies have found that meditation produces slower brain wave patterns; slower waves are normally found during sleep, yet meditators are awake and very alert.[273]

A few older EEG studies looked at Indian yogis during moments of spiritual ecstasy. In one of the earliest studies, N. N. Das and Henri Gastaut found that during moments of religious ecstasy, an Indian yogi exhibited unexpected beta waves in a specific area of his brain.[274] They described these changes as "very spectacular" modifications. Other studies have reported similar fast brain wave patterns associated with ecstasy and samadhi.

A number of studies have reported a pattern of synchronization and coherence of brain activity between hemispheres of the brain during meditation. For example, Richard Davidson and his colleagues have completed a series of interesting studies with very experienced Tibetan Buddhist monks. One of the studies involved physiological readings of eight monks who had meditated from 10,000–50,000 hours over periods of ten to forty years.[275] The study showed that during meditation, the monks could produce high-amplitude gamma waves (very fast waves, about 24–40+ Hz). In addition, the monks produced phase-synchrony of the gamma waves, which indicated more integration among different cortical areas. In fact, the most dramatic results were found with the most experienced monks. In addition, even while resting in a neutral state, the monks had higher gamma activity than the control group. This suggested that brain activity may be permanently altered through the practice of meditation. In addition, some studies suggest that long-term meditation may actually increase brain size in specific areas of the brain.[276] The assumption is that meditation stimulates the growth of more neurons in those areas.

Eugene d'Aquili and Andrew Newberg call their approach to the study of religious experiences *neurotheology*, in reference to the use of neurological imaging techniques to study religious experiences.[277] In one study, they used neuroimaging technology to record brain activity in very experienced Tibetan Buddhist monks while they were meditating. They found that cortical areas of the brain that are involved in creating a sense of self were activated during deep meditative experiences. They argued that activation of those areas could lead to a sense that the perceptual boundary between self and other was temporarily breaking down, and this would result in a feeling of oneness with the world.

Returning to research by Davidson, his studies have also found recognizable patterns of brain activity that are associated with both positive and negative moods. Specifically, when people report feeling happy, more activity is seen in the left frontal cortex. This increased activity can be seen with EEG recordings or with functional magnetic resonance imaging (fMRI), which measures blood flow in various areas of the brain as people are engaged in different tasks or are experiencing different emotions. Davidson and others have found that for most people, meditation changes brain activity toward the patterns associated with positive moods.

A study by Davidson recorded brain activity as measured by fMRI in a Tibetan Buddhist monk who had extensive experience with meditation.[278] The monk said he could voluntarily induce feelings of universal compassion during meditation. In fact, during meditation, each time the monk signaled he was entering the compassionate meditative state there were significant and consistent changes in his brain activity. Interestingly, Davidson also found that of all the people tested in his studies, the monk had the most extreme shift toward the brain pattern associated with positive emotions.

PSYCHOTHERAPY AND COUNSELING

As mentioned earlier, initial interest in Eastern psychology came primarily from a number of psychologists who practiced meditation, yoga, and other Eastern spiritual disciplines. Usually, these psychologists came from applied areas of psychology and were interested in personal growth. Therefore, when articles did appear in professional journals, they tended to be found in those affiliated with clinical and counseling psychology or psychiatry. In the early years, they were often associated with humanistic or transpersonal psychology. Since the early classic work on Zen and psychoanalysis by D. T. Suzuki, Erich Fromm, and Richard de Martino, Western psychologists and psychiatrists trained in psychotherapy have continued to write about the interface between Eastern and Western psychology. In fact, this literature is very extensive at this point. Numerous researchers and scholars have written about the advantages of meditation, yoga, tai chi chuan, and other ideas taken from Hinduism, Buddhism, and Taoism.[279] The impact of Buddhism on contemporary theories of therapy was seen when a special issue of the research journal *Cognition and Behavior Practice* was devoted specifically to the integration of cognitive-behavioral therapies and Buddhist ideas.[280]

A few contemporary forms of psychotherapy have incorporated mindfulness into their treatments. Therapies such as Dialectic Therapy and Acceptance and Commitment Therapy (ACT) make extensive use of mindfulness meditation.[281] The ideas of Buddhism have had considerable influence in ACT therapy especially. Steven Hayes, the developer of this therapy, readily acknowledges the contributions of Buddhist ideas to ACT.[282]

Transpersonal Psychotherapy Today, there are a number of Western therapists who try to bring transpersonal forms of psychotherapy into more traditional models of therapy. For example, Seymour Boorstein and William Mikulas have attempted to blend traditional psychotherapy models with transpersonal concerns.[283] In addition, practitioners of Eastern psychology have taken Eastern ideas and presented them to the general public as examples of personal and spiritual growth.[284] For instance, Ken Wilber, Terry Patten, Adam Leonard, and Marco Morelli have recently developed Wilber's developmental stages model into a system of personal and spiritual growth for a more general audience.[285] Stanislav Grof developed a method called *holotropic breathing* to help guide people through the levels of the unconscious he postulated without the use of psychedelics.[286] His method involves programmed breathing and music to naturally induce spiritual experiences. Grof was influenced by music therapist Helen Bonny, who began using programmed musical journeys a number of years ago to facilitate spiritual experiences with or without psychedelic drugs.[287] However, much of the work in transpersonal forms of therapy is quite preliminary. Not only is the research base very sparse, but the difficulties of combining very different models of mental health is all too obvious in approaches that seek to bridge substantial gaps between Eastern and Western models of personality and mental health.

RESEARCH STUDIES OF MYSTICAL EXPERIENCES

As a fair amount of writing in Eastern psychology has focused on mystical experiences, another of the unique contributions to research has been the study of mysticism. From the initial interest of William James at the very end of the nineteenth century, a number of researchers in the psychology of religion have written extensively on mysticism from a psychological point of view. Early works by James Leuba and W. T. Stace evolved into more empirical approaches such as those of Ralph Hood and the sociologist Andrew Greely. In addition to surveys and correlational analyses, there have been attempts to experimentally induce mystical experiences. Attempts to induce states similar to mystical experiences have used vehicles such as semistructured nature excursions and hypnosis.[288] Studies have also found that religious conversion experiences can alter attitudes, goals, feelings, behaviors, and life meanings, and can increase positive emotion and well-being.[289] Some of the experiences may involve spiritual epiphanies or what appear to be deep insights into a spiritual reality.

Studies of Entheogens   The most dramatic attempts to induce mystical experiences have used psychedelic drugs. The research with psychedelic drugs has been particularly successful in producing states that appear to be very similar to mystical experiences. Drugs that can induce experiences with a distinct spiritual or religious interpretation are called *entheogens*.[290]

After the late 1960s and early 1970s, research on psychedelics almost completely disappeared. However, in the past few years, a small number of studies have once again been done that investigated the impact of psychedelics on well-being and mental health. Studies have found that the careful and controlled administration of psychedelics can help people with a number of psychological problems, including obsessive-compulsive disorder, alcoholism, and post-traumatic stress disorder.[291] Psychedelic therapy can also allow terminal cancer patients to find greater meaning in life and acceptance of death.[292]

One of the most famous studies using entheogens was the "Good Friday Experiment" of Walter Panke and William Richards.[293] In this study, twenty graduate seminary students from Protestant backgrounds were randomly assigned to either take psilocybin (the psychoactive ingredient in psychedelic mushrooms) or a placebo. Both groups then listened to a Good Friday church service from a special room adjacent to the church nave. After the experience, all participants wrote descriptions of their experiences and completed a mysticism questionnaire. The researchers concluded that the written accounts of those in the psilocybin group were indistinguishable from traditional mystical experiences. A follow-up study twenty-five years later found that the participants still recalled the psilocybin experience as extremely memorable and meaningful.[294]

A recent study by Griffiths, Richards, McCann, and Jesse attempted to recreate the Good Friday experiment with better research controls and a more sophisticated research design.[295]. The results showed that 58 percent of the participants in the psilocybin sessions had experiences that were indistinguishable from meditation-induced mystical experiences. That is, responses to questionnaires indicated that they had a "complete" mystical experience. A follow-up completed fourteen months after the sessions found that an average of 62 percent of the participants rated the psilocybin sessions as among the top five most personally meaningful experiences and among the top five most spiritually significant experiences of their lives.[296] In addition, other people who knew the participants reported significant positive changes in their mood and behavior after the psilocybin sessions.

EDUCATION AND EAST-WEST PSYCHOLOGY

In terms of educating future psychologists, there has also been evidence of interest in Eastern ideas. Textbooks on personality theories have included chapters on Eastern psychology for a number of years. For instance, James Fadiman and Roger Frager published a textbook on personality theory that includes major sections on Buddhism, Hinduism, and Taoism in addition to sections on the traditional theories of Western psychology.[297] There are also entire universities that place traditional higher education in a context that is grounded in Eastern ideas. The Maharishi University of Management is founded on the practice of transcendental meditation, Naropa University is based on Tibetan Buddhist theory and practice, and both the California Institute of Integral Studies and Institute of Transpersonal Psychology are grounded in transpersonal psychology.

WESTERN PSYCHOLOGY INFLUENCES MEDITATION PRACTICE

At this time, it seems that meditation has firmly established itself in the West. Many Westerners have trained in Eastern countries under meditation masters, and there are now a number of formal ashrams, monasteries, and meditation centers in North and South America and across Europe. Interestingly, the cross-fertilization of East and West has also been seen working in the other direction—the West influencing the East. Some Western-born Zen masters, lamas, and advanced meditation teachers have begun to incorporate elements of Western psychotherapy into their training systems. For example, Zen masters Dennis Genpo Merzel and Cheri Huber have both adopted elements of Jungian therapy into their work. Psychodynamic therapists such as Mark Epstein and Barry Magid are developing styles of therapy and meditation training that combine Western and Eastern insights into human behavior.[298] In addition, elements of Western style group therapy can be seen in some contemporary meditation centers. In fact, as more Westerners become meditation masters and teachers, there is a tendency to incorporate both the language and concerns of Western psychotherapy into traditional meditation practices. Most Western-born meditation teachers have created teaching styles that are compatible with practitioners in the Western world who have grown up in a culture that is partially defined by Freud, individualism, and self-actualization.

Traditional styles of meditation practice imported to the West have also changed to fit Western ideals. For instance, most practitioners in Western cultures are lay people rather than monks. In addition, the practice of separating men and women, or monks and nuns, is common in the East but has changed so that men and women practice together in the West, and many women are meditation masters and run meditation centers.

Conclusions

The psychological systems of the East offer a rich vein of ideas and techniques for anyone interested in well-being, the human personality, and optimal states of personality. The recent explorations into this area by Western psychologists have produced an amazing variety of ideas that could be incorporated into the psychological systems of the Western world. At the same time, the priorities of Western psychology, such as scientific investigation and the search for well-being outside the context of a spiritual discipline, have helped enrich the Eastern models of well-being. It looks like the two systems have finally met, and something resembling a fruitful relationship is rapidly developing—one that should turn into a deep and lasting friendship.

Bibliography

Addis, S., & Lombardo, S. (trans.) (1993). *Lao-Tzu: Tao Te Ching*. Indianapolis, IN: Hackett.

Adler, A. (1964). *Social Interest: A challenge to mankind*. N.Y.: Capricorn (original work published 1938).

Ajaya, Swami (Ed.). (1977). *Foundations of Eastern and Western psychology*. Glenview, IL: The Himalayan Institute.

Alexander, C. N., Rainforth, M. V., & Gelderloos, P. (1991). Transcendental Meditation, self-actualization, and psychological health: A conceptual overview and statistical meta-analysis. In A. Jones & R. Crandall (Eds.), *Handbook of self-actualization* (pp. 189–248). Madera, CA: Select Press.

Algoe, S., & Haidt, J. (2009). Witnessing excellence in action: The other-praising emotions of elevation, admiration, and gratitude. *Journal of Positive Psychology, 4*, 105–127.

Arya, O. U. (trans.). (1986). *Yoga-sutras of Patanjali with exposition of Vyasa (Vol. I)*. Honesdale, PA: The Himalayan International Institute of Yoga Science and Philosophy.

Assagioli, R. (1965). *Psychosynthesis*. New York: Viking.

Austin, J. H. (1998). *Zen and the brain: Toward an understanding of meditation and consciousness.* Cambridge, MA: MIT Press.

Ball, P. (2004). *The essence of Tao.* London: Arcturus Publishing Limited.

Beck, C. J. (1989). *Everyday Zen: Love & work.* San Francisco, CA: Harper & Row.

Benson, H., Malhotra, M. S., Goldman, R. F., Jacobs, G. D., et al. (1990). Three case reports on the metabolic and electroencephalographic changes during advanced Buddhist meditation techniques. *Behavioral Medicine, 16*(2), 90–95.

Billington, R. (1997). *Understanding Eastern philosophy.* N.Y.: Routledge.

Blackmore, S. (2004). *Consciousness: An introduction.* Oxford: Oxford University Press.

Blofeld, J. (1974). *The tantric mysticism of Tibet: A practical guide.* New York: Causeway.

Boorstein, S. (Ed.). (1980). *Transpersonal psychotherapy.* Palo Alto, CA: Science & Behavior.

Boss, M. (1979). Eastern wisdom and western psychotherapy. In J. Welwood (Ed.), *Meeting of the ways: Explorations in east/west psychology* (pp. 179–182). New York: Schoken.

Bowers, D. (1973). Democratic vistas. In B. M. Barbour (Ed.), *American transcendentalism: An anthology of criticism.* Notre Dame, IN: University of Notre Dame Press.

Bowker, J. (Ed.). (1997). *The Oxford dictionary of world religions.* Oxford: Oxford University Press.

Brown, D. P. (1977). A model for the levels of concentrative meditation. *The International Journal of Clinical and Experimental Hypnosis, 25*(4), 236–273.

Brown, D. P., & Engler, J. (1980). The stages of mindfulness meditation: A validation study. *The Journal of Transpersonal Psychology, 12*(2), 143–192.

Brown, K. W., & Ryan, R. M. (2003). The benefits of being present: Mindfulness and its role in psychological well-being. *Journal of Personality and Social Psychology, 84*(4), 822–848.

Buhler, C., & Allen, M. (1972). *Introduction to humanistic psychology.* Monterey, CA: Brook/Cole.

Campos, P. (2002). Introduction. *Cognitive and Behavioral Practice [special issue on Buddhism and cognitive-behavioral therapy], 9*(1), Winter, 38–39.

Chaudhuri, H. (1975). Yoga psychology. In C. Tart (Ed.), *Transpersonal psychologies* (pp. 231–280). New York: Harper & Row.

Chen, K. (2004). An analytic review of studies on measuring effects of external *Qi* in China. *Alternative Therapies, 10*(4), 38–50.

Chirban, J. (1986). Developmental stages in Eastern Orthodox Christianity. In K. Wilber, J. Engler, & D. Brown (Eds.), *Transformations of consciousness* (pp. 285-314). Boston: Shambhala.

Cleary, T. (1991). *The essential Tao.* New York: Harper Collins.

Coan, R. W. (1977). *Hero, artist, sage, or saint*. New York: Columbia University Press.

Coleman, G., Jinpa, T., & Dorje, G. (2007). *The Tibetan book of the dead.* New York: Penguin classics.

Compton, W. C. (1982). *A relationship between self-actualization and the practice of Zen meditation.* Unpublished master's thesis, University of Nebraska at Omaha, Omaha, NE.

Compton, W. C. (1984). Meditation and self-actualization: A cautionary note on the Sallis article. *Psychologia: An International Journal of Psychology in the Orient, 27*(2), 125–127.

Compton, W. C., & Becker, G. M. (1983). Self-actualization and experience with Zen meditation: Is a learning period necessary? *Journal of Clinical Psychology, 38,* 292–296.

Compton, W. C., & Hoffman, E. (2013). *Positive psychology: The science of happiness and flourishing* (2nd ed.). Belmont, CA.: Wadsworth/Cengage Learning.

Csikszentmihalyi, M. (1997). *Finding flow: The psychology of engagement with everyday life.* New York: Basic Books.

Csikszentmihalyi, M., & Csikszentmihalyi, I. (1988). *Optimal experience: Psychological studies of flow in consciousness.* New York: Cambridge University Press.

d'Aquili, E. G., & Newberg, A. B. (1999). *The mystical mind: Probing the biology of religious experiences.* Minneapolis, MN: Fortress Press.

The Dalai Lama with Cutler, H.C. (1998). *The art of happiness: A handbook for living.* New York: Penguin.

The Dalai Lama (2005-2006). Contemplative mind, hard science. *Shift: At the Frontiers of Consciousness,* No. 9 (December 2005–January 2006), 24–27.

Danielou, A. (1994). *The complete Kama Sutra: The first unabridged modern translation of the classic Indian text.* Bethel, ME: Park Street Press.

Das, N. N., & Gastaut, H. (1955). Variations de l'activite electrique du cerveau, du coeur et des muscles squellettiques au cours de la meditation et de l'extase yogique [Variations in the electrical activity of the brain, heart, and skeletal muscles during Yogic meditation and trance]. *Electroencephalography and Clinical Neurophysiology, supplement no. 6,* 211–219.

Das, Ram. (1971). *Be here now.* New York: Three Rivers Press.

Das, Ram. (1993). *Riding the waves of change* [video tape]. Berkeley, CA: New Medicine Tapes.

Dave, J. P. (1977). Personality—the Eastern perspective. In Swami Ajaya (Ed.), *Foundations of eastern and western psychology* (pp. 54-76). Glenview, IL: The Himalayan Institute.

Davidson, R., & Harrington, A. (Eds.) (2002). *Visions of compassion: Western scientists and Tibetan Buddhists examine human nature.* New York: Oxford University Press.

Doblin, R. (1991). Pahnke's Good Friday experiment: A long-term follow-up and methodological critique. *Journal of Transpersonal Psychology, 23,* 1–28.

Ekman, P., Davidson, R. J., Ricard, M., & Wallace, B. A. (2005). Buddhist and psychological perspectives on emotions and well-being. *American Psychological Society, 14*(2), 59–63.

Eliade, M. (1972). *Shamanism: Archaic techniques of ecstasy.* Bollingen Press.

Emmons, R. A., & Paloutzian, R. F. (2003). The psychology of religion. *Annual Review of Psychology, 54,* 377–402.

Epstein, M. (1995). *Thoughts without a thinker.* New York: Basic Books.

Epstein, M. (1988). The deconstruction of the self: Ego and "egolessness" in Buddhist insight meditation. *Journal of Transpersonal Psychology, 20*(1), 61–69.

Epstein, M. (2008). *Psychotherapy without the Self: A Buddhist perspective.* New Haven, CT: Yale University Press.

Evans-Wentz, W., Lopez, D., & Jung C. (2000). *The Tibetan book of the dead.* Oxford: Oxford University Press.

Fadiman, J. & Frager, R. (1994). *Personality and personal growth* (3rd ed.). New York: Harper Collins.

Feuerstein (2003). *Yoga wisdom: Teachings on happiness, peace, and freedom* [audiotape]. Boulder, CO: Sounds True.

Fields, R., Taylor, P., Weyler, R., & Ingrasci, R. (1984). *Chop wood carry water: A guide to finding spiritual fulfillment in everyday life.* New York: St. Martin's Press.

Fisher-Schreiber, I., Ehrhard, F. K., & Diener, M. S. (1991). *The Shambhala dictionary of Buddhism and Zen* (M. H. Kohn, Trans.). Boston, MA: Shambhala.

Fiske, S. T., & Taylor, S. E. (1991). *Social cognition.* New York: McGraw-Hill.

Frankl, V. (1963). *Man's search for meaning.* New York: Pocket.

Fredrickson, B., Cohn, M., Coffey, K., Pek, J., & Finkel, S. (2008). Open hearts build lives: Positive emotions, induced through loving-kindness meditation, build consequential personal resources. *Journal of Personality and Social Psychology, 95*(5), 1045–1062.

Fromm, E. (1996). *The art of being.* New York: Continuum.

Goleman, D. (1972a). The Buddha on meditation and states of consciousness. Part I: The teachings. *Journal of Transpersonal Psychology, 7*(1), 1–44.

Goleman, D. (1972b). The Buddha on meditation and states of consciousness. Part II: A typology of meditation techniques. *Journal of Transpersonal Psychology, 7*(2), 151–210.

Goleman, D. (1981). Buddhist and western psychology: Some commonalities and differences. *Journal of Transpersonal Psychology, 13*(2), 125–136.

Goleman, D. (1988). *The meditative mind.* Los Angeles, CA: Jeremy P. Tarcher.

Goleman, D. (1975). Mental health in classical Buddhist psychology. *Journal of Transpersonal Psychology, 7*(2), 176–181.

Govinda, A. B. (1961). *The psychological attitude of early Buddhist philosophy, and its systematic representation according to Abhidhamma tradition.* London: Rider.

Green, E., & Green, A. (1989). *Beyond biofeedback.* New York: Knoll.

Grepmair, L., Mitterlehner, F., Loew, T., Bachler, E., Rother, W., et al. (2007). Promoting mindfulness in psychotherapists in training influences the treatment results of the patients: A randomized, double-blind, controlled study. *Psychotherapy and Psychosomatics, 76*, 332–338.

Griffiths, R. R., Richards, W. A., McCann, U., & Jesse, R. (2006). Psilocybin can occasion mystical-type experiences having substantial and stained personal meaning and spiritual significance. *Psychopharmacology, 187*, 268–283.

Griffiths, R., Richards, W., Johnson, M., McCann, U., & Jesse, R. (2008). Mystical-type experiences occasioned by psilocybin mediate the attribution of personal meaning and spiritual significance 14 months later. *Journal of Psychopharmacology, 22*(6), 621–632.

Grob, C. S., Danforth, A. L., Chopra, G. S., Hagerty, M., McKay, C. R., Halberstadt, A. L., Greer, G. R. (2010). Pilot study of psilocybin treatment for anxiety in patients with advanced-stage cancer. *Archives of General Psychiatry,* Sep 6.

Grof, S. (1976). *Realms of the human unconscious: Observations from LSD research.* New York: E. P. Dutton & Co.

Grof, S., & Grof, C. (1993). *Spiritual emergency: When personal transformation becomes a crisis.* New York: Putnam Books.

Grof, S., & Grof, C. (2010). *Holotropic breathwork: A new approach to self-exploration and therapy (Suny series in transpersonal and humanistic psychology).* Albany, NY: State University of New York Press.

Hagen, L. (2002). Taoism and psychology. In R. P. Olson (Ed.), *Religious theories of personality and psychotherapy: East meets West.* (pp. 141–210). New York: Haworth Press.

Hahn, Thich Nhat. (1991). *Peace is every step.* New York: Bantam.

Haidt, J. (2000). The positive emotion of elevation. *Prevention and Treatment, 3*(3).

Hall, C. S., & Lindsey, G. (1978). *Theories of Personality* (3rd ed.). New York: John Wiley.

Hayes, S. C. (2002). Buddhism and acceptance and commitment therapy. *Cognitive and Behavioral Practice, 9*(1), 58–66.

Hayes, S., Strosahl, K., & Wilson, K. (2003). *Acceptance and commitment therapy: An experiential approach to behavior change.* New York: Guilford.

Hermsen, E. (1996). Person-centered psychology and Taoism: The reception of Lao-tzu by Carl R. Rogers. *International Journal for the Study of Religion, 6*(2), 107–125.

Herrigel, E. (1999). *Zen and the art of archery.* New York: Vintage.

Hirai, T. (1974). *The psychophysiology of Zen.* Tokyo: Igaku Shoin.

Hoffman, E. (2007). *The way of splendor: Jewish mysticism and modern psychology* (25th anniversary edition). Lanham, MD: Rowman & Littlefield.

Hood, R. W., Jr. (1977). Eliciting mystical states of consciousness with semi-structured nature experiences. *Journal for the Scientific Study of Religion, 16*(2), 155–163.

Hood, R. W., Jr. (1997). The empirical study of mysticism. In B. Spilka & D. McIntosh (Eds.). *The Psychology of Religion: Theoretical Approaches* (pp. 222-232). Boulder, CO.: Westview Press.

Hood, R. W., Jr. (2005). Mystical, spiritual, and religious experiences. In R. Paloutzian & C. Park (Eds.), *Handbook of psychology of religion and spirituality* (pp. 348–364). New York: Guilford Press.

Hood, R. W., Jr., Morris, R. J., & Watson, P. J. (1993). Further factor analysis of Hood's mysticism scale. *Psychological Reports, 73,* 1176–1178.

Houston, R., & Masters, J. (1972). *The varieties of psychedelic experience: The classic guide to the effects of LSD on the human psyche.* Bethel, ME: Park Street.

Huber, C. (2005). *Unconditional self-acceptance* [CD recording]. Boulder, CO: Sounds True.

James, W. (1958). *The varieties of religious experience.* New York: Mentor (original work published 1902).

Kabat-Zinn, J. (1993). Mindfulness meditation: Health benefits of an ancient Buddhist practice. In D. Goleman & J. Gurin (Eds.), *Mind/body medicine: How to use your mind for better health* (pp. 259–275). Yonkers, NY: Consumer Reports Books.

Kabat-Zinn, J., Lipworth, L., & Burney, R. (1985). The clinical use of mindfulness meditation for the self-regulation of chronic pain. *Journal of Behavioral Medicine, 8,* 163–190.

Kabat-Zinn, J., Lipworth, L., Burney, R., & Sellers, W. (1986). Four year follow-up of a meditation-based program for the self-regulation of chronic pain: Treatment outcomes and compliance. *Clinical Journal of Pain, 2,* 159–173.

Kabat-Zinn, J., Massion, A, Kristeller, J., Peterson, L. G., Fletcher, K. E., Pbert, L., Lenderking, W. R., & Santorelli, S. F. (1992). Effectiveness of a meditation-based stress reduction program in the treatment of anxiety disorders. *American Journal of Psychiatry, 149*(7), 936–943.

Kaltenmark, M. (1969). *Lao Tzu and Taoism* (R. Greaves, Trans.). Stanford: Stanford University Press.

Kapleau, P., Ed. (1965). *The three pillars of Zen: Teaching, practice, enlightenment.* Boston: Beacon Press.

Kaptchuk, T. J. (2000). *The web that has no weaver: Understanding Chinese medicine.* New York: Contemporary Books.

Karamatsu, A. & Hirai, T. (1969). An EEG study on the Zen meditation (Zazen). *Psychologia, 12*(3–4), 205–225.

Keating, Thomas, Fr. (2009). *Intimacy with God: An introduction to centering prayer* (3rd ed.). New York: The Crossroad Publishing Company.

Keltner, D. (2009). *Born to be good: The science of a meaningful life.* New York: W. W. Norton.

Kitayma, S., Markus, H., Matsumoto, H., & Norasakkunkit, V. (1997). Individual and collective processes in the construction of the self: Self-enhancement in the United States and self-criticism in Japan. *Journal of Personality and Social Psychology, 72*(6), 1245–1267.

Kohr, R. (1977). Dimensionality of the meditative experience: A replication. *Journal of Transpersonal Psychology, 94*(2), 193–203.

Kornfield, J. (1993a). The seven factors of enlightenment. In R. Walsh & F. Vaughn (Eds.), *Paths beyond ego: The transpersonal vision* (pp. 56–59). Los Angeles, CA: J. P. Tarcher.

Kornfield, J. (1993b). *A path with heart: A guide through the perils and promises of spiritual life.* New York: Bantam.

Kornfield, J. (2008). *Wise heart: A guide to the universal teachings of Buddhist psychology.* New York: Bantam.

Krippner, S. (Ed.). (1972). The plateau experience: A. H. Maslow and others. *Journal of Transpersonal Psychology, 4*(2), 107–120.

Kubose, S., & Umemoto, T. (1980). Creativity and Zen. *Psychologia: An International Journal of Psychology in the Orient, 23*(1), 1–9.

Lazar, S., Kerr, C., Wasserman, R., Gray, J., Greve, D., Treadway, M., McGarvey, M., Quinn, B., Dusek, J., Benson, H., Rauch, S., Moore, C., & Fischl, B. (2005). Meditation experience is associated with increased cortical thickness. *Neuroreport for Rapid Communication of Neuroscience Research, 16*(17), 1893–1897.

Linehan, M. (1993). *Cognitive-behavioral treatment of borderline personality disorder.* New York: Guilford.

Ling, T. O. (1972). *A dictionary of Buddhism: A guide to thought and tradition.* New York: Scribner's.

Luders, E., Toga, A., Lepore, N., & Gaser, C. (2009). The underlying anatomical correlates of long-term meditation: Larger hippocampal and frontal volumes of grey matter. *NeuroImage, 45*(3), Apr 15, 672–678.

Lutz, A., Dunne, J., & Davidson, R. (2007). Meditation and the neuroscience of consciousness. In P. Zelazo, M. Moscovitch, & E. Thompson (Eds.), *Cambridge Handbook of Consciousness*. Cambridge, U.K.: Cambridge University Press.

Lutz, A., Greischar, L. L., Rawlings, N. B., Ricard, M., & Davidson, R. J. (2004). Long-term meditators self-induce high-amplitude gamma synchrony during mental practice. *PNAS, 101*(46), 16369–16373.

Magid, B. (2008). *Ending the pursuit of happiness: A Zen guide*. Boston: Wisdom.

Maguire, J. (2001). *Essential Buddhism: A complete guide to beliefs and practices*. New York: Pocket Books.

Maslow, A. H. (1968). *Toward a psychology of being*. New York: John Wiley & Sons.

Maslow, A. H. (1976). *Religions, values, and peak experiences*. New York: Penguin.

Maslow, A. H. (1970). *Motivation & personality* (2nd ed.). New York: Harper & Row.

Maslow, A. H. (1971). *The farther reaches of human nature*. New York: Viking.

Maslow, A. H. (1987). *Motivation & personality*, (3rd ed.). New York: Harper & Row.

May, G. G. (1983). *Will and spirit: A contemplative psychology*. New York: Harper & Row.

May, R., Angel, E., & Ellenberger, H. (Eds.). *Existence: A new dimension in psychiatry and psychology*. New York: Basic.

McNamara, W. (1975). Psychology and the Christian mystical tradition. In C. T. Tart (Ed.), *Transpersonal psychologies*. (pp. 395–436). New York: Harper & Row.

Merton, T. (2004). *The way of Chuang Tzu*. New York: New Directions Publishing.

Merton, T. (1967). *Mystics and Zen masters*. New York: Strauss, Farrar, & Giroux.

Merzel, D. G. (2007). *Big mind, big heart: Finding your way*. Salt Lake City, UT: Big Mind.

Mikulas, W. (2002). *The integrative helper: Convergence of Eastern and Western traditions*. Pacific Grove, CA: Brooks/Cole.

Muesse, M. (2003). *Great world religions: Hinduism* [audio tape]. Chantilly, VA: The Teaching Company.

Murti, T. R. V. (1960). *The central philosophy of Buddhism: A study of the Madhyamika system.* London: Allen and Unwin.

Newberg, A., d'Aquili, E., & Rause, V. (2002). *Why God won't go away: Brain science and the biology of belief.* New York: Ballantine.

Nyanaponika Thera. (1954). The heart of Buddhist meditation. Newburyport, MA: Red Wheel/Weiser.

Parrinder, G. (Ed.) (1971). *World religions from ancient history to the present.* New York: Facts on File.

Oken, B., Zajdel, D., Kishiyama, Flegak, K., Dehen, C., Haas, M., Kraemer, D., Lawrence, J., & Leyva, J. (2006). Randomized, controlled, six-month trial of yoga in healthy seniors: Effects on cognition and quality of life. *Alternative Therapies in Health and Medicine, 12*(1), 40–47.

Ornstein, R. (1975). Contemporary Sufism. In C. T. Tart (Ed.), *Transpersonal psychologies.* (pp. 353–394). New York: Harper & Row.

Osis, K., Bokert, E., & Carlson, M. (1973). Dimensions of the meditative experience. *Journal of Transpersonal Psychology, 5*(2), 109–135.

Owens, C. M. (1975). Zen Buddhism. In C. Tart (Ed.) (1975). *Transpersonal psychologies* (pp. 153–202). New York: Harper & Row.

Pahnke, W., & Richards, W. (1969). Implications of LSD and experimental mysticism. *Journal of Transpersonal Psychology, 7*(2), 69–102.

Paloutzian, R. (1981). Purpose in life and value changes following conversion. *Journal of Personality and Social Psychology, 41*(6), 1153–1160.

Murphy, M., & Donovan, S. (1997). *The physical and psychological effects of meditation: A review of contemporary research with a comprehensive bibliography 1931–1996.* Sausalito, CA: Institute of Noetic Sciences.

Murti, T. R. V. (1980). *The central philosophy of Buddhism.* London: George Allen & Unwin Ltd.

Rahula, W. (1974). *What the Buddha taught.* New York: Grove Press.

Rama, Swami. (1998). *The royal path: Practical lessons on yoga.* Honesdale: The Himalayan Institute Press.

Rama, Swami, Ballentine, R., & Ajaya, Swami. (1976). *Yoga and psychotherapy: The evolution of consciousness.* Honesdale: The Himalayan Institute Press.

Ring, K., & Valarino, E. E. (2006). *Lessons from light: What we can learn from near-death experience.* Newburyport, MA: Moment Point Press.

Roberts, T. B. (2006). *Psychedelic horizons.* Charlottesville, VA: Imprint Academic.

Robinson, R. & Johnson, W. (1977). *The Buddhist religion.* Encino, CA: Dickenson Publishing.

Rogers, C. R. (1959). A theory of therapy, personality, and interpersonal relationships as developed in the client-centered framework. In S. Koch (Ed.). *Psychology: A study of a science. Vol. III: Formulations of the person and the social context* New York: McGraw-Hill.

Rogers, C. R. (1961). *On becoming a person.* Boston: Houghton Mifflin.

Rychlak, J. (1997). *In defense of human consciousness.* Washington, DC: American Psychological Association.

Sacerdote, P. (1977). Application of hypnotically elicited mystical states of the treatment of physical and emotional pain. *International Journal of Clinical and Experimental Hypnosis, 25,* 309–324.

Sallis, J. (1982). Meditation and self-actualization: A theoretical comparison. *International Journal of Psychology in the Orient, 25*(1), 59–64.

Shapiro, D., & Walsh, R. (1984). *Meditation: Classic and contemporary perspectives.* New York: Aldine.

Shapiro, S., & Carlson, L. (2009). *The art and science of mindfulness: Integrating mindfulness into psychology and the helping professions.* Washington, DC: American Psychological Association.

Smith, H. (1976). *The forgotten truth: The primordial tradition.* New York: Harper & Row.

Smith, H. (1991). *The world's religions: Our great wisdom traditions.* San Francisco, CA: Harper Collins.

Stace, W. T. (1960). *The teachings of the mystics.* New York: New American Library.

Stark, M., & Washburn, M. (1977). Beyond the norm: A speculative model of self-realization. *Journal of Religion and Health, 16*(1), 58–68.

Suzuki, D. T. (1970). *Zen and Japanese culture.* Princeton, NJ: Princeton University Press.

Suzuki, D. T., Fromm, E., & De Martino, R. (1960). *Zen Buddhism and psychoanalysis*. New York: Harper & Row.

Tarnas, R. (1991). *The passion of the Western mind: Understanding the ideas that have shaped our world view*. New York: Ballantine.

Tart, C. T. (Ed.). (1969). *Altered states of consciousness*. New York: John Wiley.

Tart, C.T. (Ed.) (1975). *Transpersonal psychologies*. New York: Harper & Row.

Tigunait, P. R. (1983). *Seven systems of Indian philosophy*. Honesdale: The Himalayan Institute Press.

Thomas, C. A. (2006). *At Hell's gate: A soldier's journey from war to peace*. Boston, MA: Shambhala.

Toropov, B., & Hansen, C. (2002). *The complete idiot's guide to Taoism*. Indianapolis, IN: Alpha Books.

Trungpa, C. (1973). *Cutting through spiritual materialism*. Berkeley, CA: Shambhala Publications.

Trungpa, C. (1976). *The myth of freedom and the way of meditation*. Berkeley, CA: Shambhala.

Underhill, E. (1990). *Mysticism*. New York: Image Books.

Valle, R., & Halling, S. (1989). *Existential-phenomenological perspectives in psychology*. New York: Plenum.

Wallace, B. A., & Shapiro, S. L. (2006). Mental balance and well-being: Building bridges between Buddhism and Western psychology. *American Psychologist, 61*(7), 690–701.

Waley, A. (1958). *The way and its power*. San Francisco, CA: Grove Press.

Walsh, R. (1980). The consciousness disciplines and the behavioral sciences: Questions of comparison and assessment. *American Journal of Psychiatry, 137*(6), 663–673.

Walsh, R. (1988). Two Asian psychologies and their implications for Western psychotherapists. *American Journal of Psychotherapy, 42(4)*, 543-560.

Walsh, R. (1999). Asian contemplative disciplines: Common practices, clinical applications, and research findings. *Journal of Transpersonal Psychology, 31*(2), p. 83–107.

Walsh, R., & Vaughn, F. (1980). *Beyond ego: Transpersonal dimensions in psychology*. Los Angeles, CA: Tarcher.

Watts, A. W. (1953). *The way of Zen*. New York: Vintage.

Watts, A. W. (1968). *The meaning of happiness.* New York: Harper & Row.

Watts, A. W. (1961). *Psychotherapy East and West.* New York: Vintage.

Westkott, M. (1998). Horney, Zen and the real self. *The American Journal of Psychoanalysis, 58*(3), 287–301.

Wilber, K. (1977). *The spectrum of consciousness.* Wheaton, IL: Quest.

Wilber, K. (2000). *Integral psychology: Consciousness, spirit, psychology, therapy.* Boston, MA: Shambhala.

Wilber, K., Patten, T., Leonard, A., & Morelli, M. (2008). *Integral life practice.* Boston, MA: Shambhala.

Wilber, K., Engler, J., & Brown, D. P. (1986). *Transformations of consciousness.* Boston, MA: Shambhala.

Wilhelm, R., Bayes, C., & Jung, C. (1967). *The I Ching or book of changes (Bollingen Series XIX).* Princeton, NJ: Princeton University Press.

Wilhelm, R., & Jung, C. (1962). *The secret of the golden flower.* New York: Mariner.

Woods, R. (Ed.) (1980). *Understanding mysticism.* New York: Image Books.

Wong, E. (1997). *The Shambhala Guide to Taoism.* Boston, MA: Shambhala Publications

Wulff, D. (2004). Mystical experience. In L. Cardena & S. Krippner (Eds.), *Varieties of anomalous experience: Examining the scientific evidence* (pp. 397-440). Washington, DC: American Psychological Association.

ENDNOTES

1. Dalai Lama & H. Cutler (1998).
2. From *The Ballad of East and West*, by Rudyard Kipling.
3. For alternate dates see: http://www.buddhanet.net/e-learning/history/b_chron-txt.htm.
4. For example see: Kitayama, Markus, Matsumoto, & Norasakkunkit (1997).
5. see Goleman (1981); Walsh (1980); Watts (1961).
6. Tingunait (1983).
7. Thanks to Dr. Susan Schoenbohm for this comment.
8. Ibid.
9. Compton & Hoffman (2013).
10. See: Tart (1975); Wilber (2000).
11. Blackmore (2004); Rychlak (1997).
12. Ibid.
13. Ling (1972).
14. Tart (1969), pp. 14–15.
15. Alexander, Rainforth, & Gelderloos (1991).
16. Govinda (1961).
17. Eliade(1972)
18. Woods (1980).
19. Ibid.
20. see Emmons & Paloutzian (2003).
21. Hood (2005); Wulff (2004).
22. Eva Wong (1997)
23. Stace, 1960; Wulff (2004).
24. Hood et al. (1993).
25. Tigunait (1983), p. 218.
26. Rama (1998), p. 123.
27. Ram Das (1993).
28. Merton (1965), p. 40.
29. Govinda (1961), p. 4.
30. Tart (1975); Underhill (1990).
31. Merton (1967).
32. Hoffman (2007).
33. Ornstein (1975).

34. Govinda (1961).

35. Fiske & Taylor(1991).

36. Kaptchuk (2000), pp. 14–15.

37. Ibid, p.15.

38. Hagen (2002), p. 141.

39. Some readers may notice that Eastern concepts such as the Tao are similar to the idea of "the Force" in the Star Wars movies. Anyone familiar with the Star Wars movies will recognize many of the qualities associated with the enlightened sage in Taoism. In those movies, Jedi masters have learned to harness the energy of the Force, which allows them to control aspects of both psychological and physical reality. Jedi masters can harness natural forces such as gravity, can influence the thoughts of others, and have mastered their own internal demons to achieve inner peace. In fact, George Lucas, the creator of those movies, drew heavily from Eastern ideas for his movies. The writings of Taoism are filled with images of sages performing identical feats—although there is certainly a metaphorical element to these writings. These same ideas are seen in a more fanciful form in many Asian martial arts movies.

40. Muesse (2003).

41. Ibid; Parrinder (1971).

42. Tigunait (1983), pp. 10–11.

43. Mascaro (1965).

44. Mascaro (1962).

45. Muesse (2003).

46. Smith (1991), p. 27.

47. Arya, O. U. (trans.) (1986). *Yoga-Sutras of Patanjali with Exposition of Vyasa* (Vol. I). Honesdale, Pennsylvania: The Himalayan International Institute of Yoga Science and Philosophy.

48. Feuerstein (2003).

49. This date was taken from Robinson & Johnson (1977). Scholars differ on exactly what these dates should be. For alternate dates, see: http://www.buddhanet.net/e-learning/history/b_chron-txt.htm.

50. http://www.tricycle.com/feature/whose-buddhism-truest

51. Luk (1984).

52. Other significant schools of Buddhism found today include Tendai, Shingon, Nichiren, and Pure-land. Tendai is one of the oldest schools

that originated in China. It is an esoteric school with teachings based on the Lotus Sutra. Shingon Buddhism is a school that blends elements of both Zen and Tibetan Buddhism. Pure-land Buddhism focuses on chanting the name of the Buddha and nurturing a deep faith that one will be reborn in the Pure Land. Nichiren Buddhism is also based on the Lotus Sutra and also uses chanting as the main practice. A number of western celebrities, such as Tina Turner, follow this school. See www.bbc.co.uk/religion/religions/buddhism/index.shtml and Yu (1984).

53. Maguire (2001).

54. Wong (1997).

55. Ibid, p.23.

56. Smith (1991), p.198.

57. Taoism is sometimes spelled as it sounds in English ("Daoism"). Some contemporary scholars prefer the spellings that are used today by native speakers of Chinese. For example, Lao-tzu: Laozi, Tao Te Ching: Daode Jing, Chuang-Tzu: Zhuangzi (see Toropov and Hansen, 2002).

58. Wong (1997).

59. Dalai Lama (2005–2006). Contemplative mind, hard science. *Shift: At the Frontiers of Consciousness*, No. 9 (December 2005–January 2006), pp. 24–27.

60. Tingunait (1983), p.26.

61. Smith (1991), pp. 21, 25.

62. Murti (1980).

63. Ibid.

64. Rahula (1974).

65. Wong (1997), p. 23.

66. Mitchell (1988), p. 11.

67. Addis & Lombardo (1993), p. 4.

68. See Wong (1997) pp. 124–131 for an explanation of the cosmological significance of this and other Taoist symbols.

69. Kaltenmark (1969), p. 24.

70. Ibid, p.133.

71. Tigunait (1983) provides short descriptions of how the concept of God is used in various systems of Indian philosophy, including Buddhism.

72. Smith (1991), p. 2.

73. Ibid, p. 66.

74. Kwan-yin is referred to as Guanyin in China; in Tibet she is a form of Tara; the Japanese call her either Kannon or Kanzeon; and other spellings also exist.

75. Note that many gods of Hinduism have both a benign and a destructive aspect associated with them. This seems to symbolically reflect an understanding of the complex and sometimes paradoxical nature of the human personality.

76. Mascaro (1962); Parrinder(1971); Meusse (2003).

77. Kaltenmark (1969), p. 86.

78. Smith (1991), p. 72.

79. Smith (1991).

80. Robinson & Johnson (1977).

81. "Emptiness" by Thanissaru Bhikku (thanks to Lisa Ernst of One Dharma of Nashville, TN.)

82. Magid (2008), p. 22.

83. Watts (1953), p. 755.

84. Gerald May (1983), pp. 53–54.

85. from: Smith (1991).

86. In Zen, the initial taste of enlightenment is called "kensho." Subsequent, deeper experiences lead to "satori" and eventually to "great satori."

87. Fisher-Schreiber, et al. (1991).

88. Ling (1972).

89. Rahula (1974), p. 43.

90. Watts (1968), p. 65.

91. Maguire (2001).

92. Owens (1975), p. 156.

93. Ball (2004).

94. Hagen (2002), p. 143.

95. Smith (1991), p. 208

96. Kaltenmark (1969).

97. Rahula (1974), p. 37.

98. Epstein (1995), p. 98.

99. Grof & Grof (1993).

100. A person who has had an enlightenment experience or has achieved a high stage of spiritual development is referred to as a *saint* in Hinduism, a *sage* in Taoism, and a *rinpoche* in Tibetan Buddhism. Terms that are used for experienced spiritual teachers are *guru* in Hinduism, *roshi* in Zen Buddhism, and *lama* in Tibetan Buddhism.
101. Goleman (1988), pp. 137–139.
102. Interestingly, among some scholars there is speculation that the Buddha is listed among the Catholic saints as Saint Josaphat. See Maguire (2001).
103. Bowker (1997).
104. Kornfield (1993).
105. Hagen (2002), p. 161.
106. Stark and Washburn (1977).
107. Watts (1968), pp. 64–65.
108. Govinda (1961), pp. 43–44.
109. Watts (1968), p. 65.
110. Trungpa (1973).
111. See Kapleau (1965).
112. Fields, et al. (1984).
113. Beck (1989).
114. Smith (1976), p. 155.
115. de Silva (1979).
116. Compton (1984).
117. Paul Fleischman (1986), pp. 20–21.
118. *The Way of Chuan Tzu, trans.* Thomas Merton (2004), p. 76.
119. Bowker (1997), p. 803.
120. Rahula (1974).
121. Tigunait (1983), p. 24.
122. Billington (1997), p. 38.
123. Danielou (1994).
124. From the Theravada text, "The Questions of Milinda": see Maguire (2001), p. 89.
125. Ball (2004), p. 27.
126. Smith (1991), p. 28.
127. Goleman (1988).
128. Kornfield (2008)
129. Tigunait (1983), pp. 235–240.

130. Ibid.
131. Rama (1998), p. 75.
132. Georg Feuerstein (2003) notes that it is an unfortunate practice in the West to associate very specific psychological characteristics with each chakra. While each chakra can be associated with certain emotional responses, the chakras are more complex than these simple emotional associations.
133. Rama et al. (1976).
134. Kundalini, en.wikipedia.org/wiki/Kundalini#Personal_testimonies
135. Ajaya (1977), p. 67.
136. Feuerstein (2003).
137. The development of tantra in about the 8th C. also viewed the body as a potential "launching pad" for spiritual development.
138. Trungpa (1973).
139. Kornfield (2008).
140. Trungpa (1973, 1976).
141. http://webspace.ship.edu/cgboer/buddhapers.html.
142. Robinson & Johnson (1977).
143. Chogyam Trungpa (1976), pp. 23–40, presents an engaging psychological description of the six realms.
144. Trungpa (1973).
145. Robinson & Johnson (1977).
146. Rahula (1974).
147. Ibid, p. 54.
148. Kaltenmark (1969), p. 123.
149. Hagen (2002). p. 159.
150. Ball, (2004), p. 149.
151. In Chinese medicine, there are a number of energy meridians that travel throughout the body. The practice of acupuncture is based on the manipulation of energy in these meridians.
152. The descriptions of the energy centers are taken from Eva Wong (1997) and Lu K'uan Yu (Charles Luk) (1973).
153. Wilhelm & Jung (1962).
154. Yang, Jwing-Ming (1997).
155. Yu (1973).
156. See Alexander, Rainforth, & Gelderoos (1991).
157. Ram Das (1993).

158. Kapleau (1965).
159. *The Royal Path: Practical Lessons on Yoga,* Swami Rama (1998), p. 115.
160. "Roshi" is a formal title given to Zen meditation masters who have experienced satori, or enlightenment.
161. Kapleau (1965).
162. Compton (1984).
163. Walsh, (1999).
164. Medard Boss (1979), p. 186.
165. Rama (1998), p.6.
166. In psychoanalytic thought, a transference reaction is a highly charged emotional reaction to another person, based not on reality but on unfulfilled needs and unresolved issues with others from the past.
167. Rahula (1974); Smith (1991).
168. Shapiro (1984), p. 6.
169. Rama (1998); Tigunait (1983).
170. Feuerstein (2003).
171. Rama (1998), p. 13.
172. The interested reader should consult Rahula (1974) and Murti (1980) for a more comprehensive presentation of Buddhist philosophy. The classic "textbook" of Buddhist psychology is the *Abhidhamma.* Govinda's (1974) treatment of this work is most helpful. Nyanaponika (1954) covers Buddhist meditation.
173. Salzberg & Goldstein (1996).
174. Rahula (1974).
175. Ibid, p. 17.
176. Mark Epstein (1995), p. 48.
177. McGuire (2001).
178. Kornfield (1993).
179. Hermsen (1996).
180. Cleary (1991), p. 9.
181. Smith (1991), p. 204.
182. Ibid, p. 208.
183. In Western traditions, prayer can be a form of meditation. Father Thomas Keating's use of Centering Prayer is a perfect example.
184. Goleman (1988).
185. McGuire (2001), p. 121.
186. See Wallace & Shapiro (2006), p. 696.

187. One of the many logical paradoxes of Eastern psychology found by asking, "Who is it that observes this dissolution of the self?"
188. Rahula (1974).
189. Goleman (1988).
190. A study I did with practitioners of Zen meditation found that increases in self-actualization were not apparent until after at least thirteen months of practice (Compton & Becker, 1984). We attributed this to the initial difficulty of insight meditation.
191. The description of meditation stages is taken from Goleman (1988) and Brown (1977).
192. Rama (1998), p. 5.
193. Ibid, p. 5
194. Govinda (1961).
195. Ibid.
196. Goleman (1988), p. 18.
197. Wallace & Shapiro (2006).
198. Goleman (1988), pp. 20–21.
199. Nyanaponika, quoted in Wlbur, Engler & Brown (1986), p. 20.
200. Goleman (1988), p. 26.
201. Woods (1980).
202. The descriptions of the stages is taken from Eva Wong (1997).
203. Yu (1984), pp. 205–207.
204. Ibid.
205. Goleman (1988).
206. Hahn (1991).
207. Zen monk Claude Anshin Thomas (2006) has done extensive walking meditation across Europe, the United States, and other countries. On these journeys, he has covered thousands of miles with virtually no possessions other than a blanket.
208. On Reek or Garland Sunday, some devout Irish Catholics will walk up Croagh Patrick, a mountain in County Mayo, Ireland. Many walk barefoot over the sharp rocks as a pilgrimage to the top, where St. Patrick is said to have once built a church.
209. Kornfield (1993), pp. 19–21.
210. Western religious music also has a very rich tradition. Anyone wishing to experience the ability of music to express spirituality has options ranging from Gregorian Chant to hymns to a wide variety of classical composers

through the centuries. In San Francisco, California, a small group of people recently formed the Church of John Coltrane. They use the music of this famous jazz musician to express a deep spirituality.

211. Herrigel (1999).
212. Suzuki (1970).
213. Green & Green (1989).
214. Cleary (trans, 1996).
215. Rama, Ballantine & Ajaya (1976).
216. Ibid.
217. Wong (1997).
218. http://news.harvard.edu/gazette/2002/04.18/09-tummo.html
219. Coleman, Jinpa & Dorje (2007); also spelled *Bardo Todrol*.
220. Ring (1980).
221. Kapleau (1965), pp. 252–254. Note: I have edited this quote due to space limitations.
222. Kubose & Umemoto (1980).
223. Unlike the other Chinese terms in the text, "Qigong" is written using the Chinese spelling. This is because the Chinese spelling is more commonly used in the West.
224. Yang, Jwing-Ming (1997).
225. Tai chi chuan is actually a martial art designed to help people defend themselves. My tai chi chuan teacher has frequently stated that many martial arts instructors consider tai chi to be the "most effective" martial art. However, it is also "the least practical," because it takes at least thirty years to develop the necessary skill to use it for defense. On the other hand, the benefits of tai chi chuan can be felt quite quickly when it is used as meditation and a form of exercise.
226. Kornfield, J. (2010). http://www.inquiringminds.com/Articles/Enlightenments.
227. Quoted in Wilber(1977), p. 38.
228. Tarnas (1991).
229. Woods (1980); http://www.religiousworlds.com/mystic/whoswho.html.
230. Honderich (1995).
231. Bowers (1973) p. 16.
232. Ibid., p. 17.
233. James (1902, 1958), p. 298.
234. Evans-Wentz, Lopez & Jung (2000); Wilhelm, Baynes, Eber, & Jung (1995); Wilhelm & Jung (1962).

235. Assagioli (1965); Coan (1977).

236. Westkott (1998).

237. Suzuki, Fromm & DeMartino (1960).

238. Fromm (2005).

239. Hermsen (1996).

240. Maslow (1954).

241. Maslow (1968).

242. Sallis (1982), but also see Compton (1983) and Murphy & Donovan (1997) for research studies on meditation and self-actualization; those really interested in the topic may want to hunt up Compton (1982).

243. Maslow (1976).

244. Maslow (1987), p. 163.

245. Maslow (1970).

246. Keltner (2009).

247. see Krippner (1972); Maslow (1970); Cleary & Shapiro (1995).

248. May, Angel, & Ellenberger (1958).

249. Frankl (1963).

250. Csikszentmihalyi (1990; 1997)

251. Comments made by Dainin Katagiri-Roshi.

252. Maslow (1968).

253. Valle & Halling (1989).

254. Grof (1996). See also Houston & Masters (1972) who had earlier conceptualized a stage model for the depth of psychedelic experiences that was quite similar to Grof's.

255. See *The Collected Works of Ken Wilber* at Shambhala publications.

256. Wallace & Shapiro (2006).

257. Ekman (2005).

258. Davidson & Harrington (2002).

259. Hood (1997).

260. Murphy & Donovan (1997); Shapiro & Walsh (1984).

261. http://www.tm.org/research-on-meditation; Orme-Johnson & Farrow (1977).

262. Hirai (1974); Murphy & Donovan (1997); Shapiro & Carson (2009).

263. Murphy & Donovan (1997).

264. Osis, Bokert, and Carlson (1973); Kohr (1977).

265. Kohr (1977), p. 27.

266. Brown & Engler (1984, 1986).

267. Fredrickson, Cohn, Coffey, Pek, & Finkel (2008).

268. For example: Oken, Zajdel, Kishiyama, Flegel, Dehen, et al. (2006); Chen (2004).

269. Shapiro & Carlson (2009).

270. Grepmair, Mitterlehner, Loew, Bachler, Rother, et al. (2009).

271. Austin (1998); Lutz, Dunne, & Davidson (2007).

272. Benson, Malhotra, Goldman, & Jacobs (1990).

273. Karamarsu & Harai (1966); see Murphy & Donovan (1997).

274. Das & Gastaut (1955).

275. Lutz, Greischer, Rawlings, Ricard, & Davidson (2004).

276. Lazar, Kerr, Wasserman, Grey, Greve, et al. (2005); Luders et al. (2009).

277. d'Aquili & Newberg (1999); Newberg, d'Aquili & Rouse (2001).

278. Lutz, Greischer, Rawlings, Ricard, & Davidson (2004).

279. See Brown (1977); Epstein (1995); Goleman (1981); Walsh (1988); Walsh & Vaughn (1980).

280. Campos (2002).

281. Linehan (1993); Hayes, Strosahl, & Wilson (1993).

282. Hayes (2002).

283. Boorstein (1980); Mikulas (2002).

284. See the works of Pema Chodron – an American born Tibetan Buddhist nun who blends Buddhist teachings with Western psychology into a compassionate and meticulous presentation.

285. Wilber, Patten, Leonard & Morelli (2008).

286. Grof & Grof (2010).

287. www.ami-bonnymethod.org/bonnyinstitute.asp

288. Hood (1977); Sacerdote (1977).

289. Beit-Hallahmi & Argyle (1997); McCullough (1995); Paloutzian, Richardson & Rambo (1999); Greely (1975), reported in Argyle (1999).

290. Roberts, T. (2006).

291. Richards (1978); news.bbc.co.uk/1/hi/health/3528730.stm

292. Marsa (2008).

293. Panke & Richards (1969).

294. Doblin (1991).

295. Griffiths, Richards, McCann & Jesse (2006).

296. Griffiths, Richards, Johnson, McCann & Jesse (2008).

297. Fadiman & Frager (1994); see also Hall & Lindsey (1978).

298. Epstein (2008); Huber (2005); Magid (2008); Merzel (2007).

Index

Made in the USA
Coppell, TX
11 September 2020

37628729R00115